MADE IN THE IMAGE OF GOD

UNDERSTANDING THE NATURE OF GOD AND
MANKIND IN A CHANGING WORLD

Third Revised Edition

Reid A. Ashbaucher

Reid Ashbaucher Publications
Cleveland, Tennessee U.S.A.

Reid Ashbaucher Publications
Cleveland, Tennessee U.S.A.
https://ra-publications.us

MADE IN THE IMAGE OF GOD
Understanding the Nature of God and Mankind in a Changing World

Third Revised Edition

Copyright © 2011, 2016, 2017. 2020 by Reid A. Ashbaucher
All rights reserved.

No part of this publication may be reproduced, stored in a retrieval system, or transmitted in any form or by any means electronic, mechanical, photocopying, recording, or otherwise, without the prior written permission of the author.

All Scripture quotations taken from the New American Standard Bible® (NASB), Copyright © 1960, 1962, 1963, 1968, 1971, 1972, 1973, 1975, 1977, 1995 by the Lockman Foundation, unless otherwise noted. Used by permission. www.Lockman.org.

HOLY BIBLE, NEW INTERNATIONAL VERSION ® Copyright © 1973, 1978, 1984 by International Bible Society. Used by permission of Zondervan Publishing House. All rights reserved.

Scriptures taken from the King James Version of the Bible.

Reprinted by permission. "Vine's Expository Dictionary of Old Testament Words," Vine, W. E.; Unger, Merrill F.; White, William; Copyright © 1985, Thomas Nelson Publishers Inc. Nashville, Tennessee. All rights reserved.

Copyright © 1989 Warren W. Wiersbe. **"The Bible Exposition Commentary: New Testament"**. Published by David C. Cook. Published permission required to reproduce. All rights reserved.

The New Unger's Bible Dictionary. Originally published by Moody Bible Institute of Chicago, Illinois. Copyright © 1957, 1961, 1966, 1985, 1988. Used by permission.

Copyright © permissions can be obtained from the author through the following website: http://booksite.rcetc.com

Cover image by Evgeni Tcherkasski from Pixabay.com

Library of Congress Control Number: 2020932864
ISBN: 978-1-7331399-6-0 (pbk)
ISBN: 978-1-7331399-7-7 (eBook)

Printed in the United States of America
U.S. Printing History

First Edition: May 2011
Revised Edition: October 2016
Second Revised Edition: July 2017
Third Revised Edition: February 2020

TABLE OF CONTENTS

Forward ix
Preface of Third Revised Edition xi
Introduction xiii

PART ONE: THE IMAGE OF GOD
1. Key Concepts Required for Understanding this Book 19
2. The Nature of God 31
3. The Personhood of God 63
4. The Unity of God 79

PART TWO: THE IMAGE OF MANKIND
5. The Nature of Mankind 97
6. The Personhood of Mankind 111

PART THREE: MANKIND MADE IN THE IMAGE OF GOD
7. The Likeness And Image Of Mankind 141
8. Jesus Christ Both God and Man 153

APPENDICES: WORD STUDY DATA—SOUL/SPIRIT
Appendix A 183
Appendix B 193
Appendix C 203
Appendix D 217

Scripture Index 221
Acknowledgements 231
About the Author 233

Forward

On the same day I completed my initial reading of Reid Ashbaucher's book, *Made In the Image of God*, I was struck by a passage that seemed to sum up the intent and purpose of the book: Jeremiah 9:24 reads, "… But let him who boasts boast of this, that he understands and knows Me…" More than anything else, this fine book seeks to lead the reader to increase their desire and pursuit to know God.

This study of the nature of God, the Creator and man His creation made in His likeness, stresses the discipline of searching the Scriptures to understand fully what, in fact, has already been revealed. The author operates under the presumption that the subject is approachable, there is much to be known that has been revealed in God's Word, and the effort is well worth the time. The desire of the author seems to be that this knowledge leads to love, devotion and committed Christian living, assuming, as we know God more fully, we can love and worship Him more deeply.

I have known and enjoyed Christian friendship and fellowship with Reid Ashbaucher since we were seniors in high school. From the beginning of our acquaintance, we enjoyed lengthy discussions about things that really mattered, centered around our faith and the Scriptures. This book is his nature of searching things out, following his natural curiosity, looking for order, and then breaking down the complex and sharing the results with others. His respect for the Scriptures is immense, and his care in handling them wisely and respectfully is evident throughout all the pages of this work. His formal education has supplemented a love of God, His Word, and a life carefully lived since his youth.

I appreciated the systematic and logical approach taken in this book. Background information is provided when necessary, presumptions are identified, and complex concepts are clearly defined, explained, and then connected. The progression of thought is understandable, clear, and supplemented by helpful diagrams. The motivated student will find the material, although not a simple read, to be very manageable because of the logical building block approach to the study.

The author has the ability to enable the reader to get their arms around abstractions instead of running from them. I found the book to demystify effectively the area of Christian metaphysics and provide a working foundation for unintimidated further study.

The author is careful to clearly point out his chosen rules of interpretation, or hermeneutics, as he relates to the subject matter as presented in Scripture. A refreshing aspect of this book is the quantity of Scripture, not only referenced but also quoted in its entirety. There is also an extensive and very helpful index of Scripture references. The author's reliance, respect, and love for the written Word is contagious, and it is easy to get carried away reading through the passages referenced.

This book is not written for the theologian, but I think it will be seriously read by them and ultimately helpful, as it addresses the drive of every true theologian, which is to know God in a fuller and deeper way. There is another audience that will greatly appreciate the information and concepts presented—those interested in apologetics. The material presented, although not expressly intended to be, is among the best defenses I have ever read of the triune nature of God. Many will find this study lends itself to small-group Bible studies or discipleship classes in local churches. The study of this doctrine of the nature of both the Creator and the creation puts this truth on the lower shelf, making it accessible, without diminishing the great wealth of these doctrines.

I was especially benefited by the discussions of the personhood of God as Father, Son, and the Holy Spirit. The distinction the author drew from Scripture regarding the spirit of God, shared by all three persons of the Godhead, as distinct from the person of the Holy Spirit, was very helpful to me as I read many of the referenced passages and recalled my previous study of the Lord as revealed in many of the familiar Old Testament passages.

I plan to re-read this challenging book and utilize the concepts and ideas presented to further my study of the nature of God and how I, as His creation, can better relate to honor and serve Him. This book did not attempt to understand God by minimizing Him in any way, but gave me a clear windowpane to peer through and marvel at the magnificence of a God that is so indescribably great.

Respectfully,
Mark D. Yates, CPA

PREFACE OF THIRD REVISED EDITION

The Third Revised Edition is a reprint of the Second Revised Edition, with cover and minor syntax changes.

The Revised Edition, which came five years after the First Edition, was revised not for the purpose of changes in conclusions, but for better clarity to the understanding of the conclusions drawn. Within the revised edition, there have been added a few segments and comments to support and clarify the concepts being expressed, along with some minor syntax changes to help the readability and flow of the book. It should be noted that nowhere within the revised editions has there been any change in conclusions made on major concepts presented. All changes made have been for the purpose of bringing better clarity to or strengthening the arguments of the subject matters being discussed.

More than 34 years ago, I conducted a biblical word study on the terms "soul" and "spirit," then turned the work in for a grade towards my B.A. degree in Bible. Little did I know at the time that this study would become a lifelong meditation and study in my life. As I pursued my Master's degree, I majored in Theology with an emphasis on Metaphysics. Why? Because the study I started over 34 years ago, became the most important study of my life, and I needed the additional study and tools to develop the topic that raised so many practical and theological issues.

Within my studies, which included Systematic Theology, Philosophical Theology, Contemporary Theology, and World Religions that presented religions with a pluralistic world and life view, I ran across many prominent authors within the world of religion and philosophy that contributed to the topic of Religion and, subsequently, Metaphysics. These men contributed works between the seventeenth to the twentieth centuries—men like Immanuel Kant, John Locke, John Tillotson, John Toland, David Hume, Charles Darwin, Albrecht Ritschl, Charles Hodge, Thomas Aquinas, Soren Kierkegaard, Karl Barth, Paul Tillich, Reinhold Niebuhr, Karl Rahner, Jurgen Moltmann, Schubert Ogden and Rudolf Bultmann, to mention a few.

Pursuing my studies that encountered the thoughts of these men and others, I discovered that the topic of metaphysics was so widely varying and diverse, that how the world could be so confused on such a topic was not surprising to me at all. It was during this time in my studies that I knew I needed to contribute some clarity to the topic by incorporating my study of 27 years into the arena of what I term "Biblical Metaphysics."

If you are looking for a summary statement to this book, by design you will not find one. Summaries without background or study will lead to discussions without understanding; thus, such a summary would ultimately lead to the misunderstanding of this book.

I invite you to come join me for a discussion about God the creator, and how we as human beings are made in his image—a topic that is at times technical in nature, but all the same, has changed my life in how I view God, and others, within a changing world that is pluralistic in its approach to God.

If you would like to know more about God, and how this topic relates to you, I encourage you to start by reading the introduction page; it really is the starting point in this book.

INTRODUCTION

You may ask, "What is this book about and what will be discussed"? Those are fair questions. Have you ever wondered who God is? How he could be all that he claims to be, such as all-powerful, all knowing and invisible, yet exists in the person of Jesus Christ? How about God, indwelling believers, yet talks about heaven as his home—does any of this make sense to you? How is it that God is one, yet is represented as three persons? Moreover, what does Scripture really mean when it states that we are made in the image of God?

Within these pages, it is not my intent to document the world's great philosophers and their views on the subject of metaphysics, for that will be left for another book. Yet we cannot ignore the subject. Consequently, we shall cover, in brief, some background and context on the concept of metaphysics as it relates to our practical and theological discussion on the nature of things. Within all this, it is my desire to present this discussion to anyone with an interest in having a deeper knowledge of God the creator, and for those that have studied the Scriptures, but may have never pursued a degree in religion, Bible or theology. Ultimately, this discussion is for those who have sought to live their lives in the everyday world with God in mind and who would like a deeper understanding of God through scriptural study and contemplation of the God who created all things. To these and anyone else with interest, I would like to introduce the God of the Holy Scriptures—the Bible, in terms never thought of before, ultimately in hopes to aid our understanding to the concept of who God is, and how we, as his created beings, relate to him physically, emotionally, and spiritually—answering the ultimate questions: how we are alike and different with respect to the God of this universe, as he has designed it to be.

As we contemplate these concepts and questions, a biblical discussion will take place between these pages, and hopefully, those who choose to read on will walk away with a sense of understanding and awe of the great God of this universe as you contemplate life and his presence in the world.

Some may still be wondering, what relational value has this book to offer to my life? Consider the following: Is it easier to talk to someone you know? Allow me to introduce to you the God of the Bible, the creator of all things. If you could understand the nature of God and his power, would it be easier for you to believe his claims, and act on them by faith? If you understood the nature of mankind and how God relates to his creation, would it be easier to relate to your fellow man and to God? If you had a better understanding of your own nature and how that relates to God, would that draw you closer to a personal God who cares and loves you? If you had a better understanding of the God of this universe, would you have more trust for the one who cares for your soul?

It is these and many other questions of theology that this book addresses for those that are seeking. I wish I could state all the benefits that this book will contribute to your Christian life. But the benefits are all dependent on what you are looking for and what kind of answers you seek. This varies with each person. What I can say is this: After coming to the understanding of the many concepts in this book, I have greatly expanded my understanding of what I see and read in the Scriptures, which has given me a deeper fellowship, appreciation and love for my God the creator, and the lover of our souls.

Throughout the discussions in this book, remember that although this book will be analyzing God in a technical way for the purpose of clarity and understanding of his nature, God should always be seen and understood as the eternal creator of our universe, who is Holy, righteous, all-powerful and loving toward his creation. It is not my intent, through authoring these pages, to diminish God as a person(s) or as deity, or to create in your mind that somehow God is less than he claims to be, or that he is anything but the true and living God, the creator of our universe and the lover of our souls.

Some advice as to how to approach this book: It is highly recommended that you read this book from beginning to end without skipping between the pages, lest you miss the many invaluable and important concepts that will build on each other as the book progresses. Each chapter will raise new questions, which will be answered as you progress through the book—thus the benefit in following my advice not to skip any pages as you read these chapters. Some concepts have taken me more than 25 years to develop and are new and very important; if you miss them, you may ultimately be lost in how the conclusions were drawn, thus never really coming to an understanding of all that will be presented to you here within these pages.

Finally, as you read these pages, you will see a great deal of Scriptures referenced throughout this book for support of our discussion. For your convenience, these Scriptures are compiled in the Scripture Index feature of this book. In an attempt to keep this book to a length that is reasonable, we will only be discussing a small percentage of Scriptures noted throughout the book. Therefore, I highly recommend, as your curiosity arises, to look up these Scriptures as you read along, and see how they fit into the discussion. For it is the Scriptures that are truly the foundational support of all that we are trying to say.

So come, join me for chapter one, and let us get started.

PART ONE:
THE IMAGE OF GOD

Chapter One

KEY CONCEPTS REQUIRED FOR UNDERSTANDING THIS BOOK

Understanding any subject requires some basic knowledge or foundation to build on. For example, in mathematics we start by learning our numbers, then how those numbers relate to each other, and then how to use those numbers to achieve a goal. As we advance, we move into higher math, starting with Algebra, then Geometry, and on to Trigonometry and so on. The subject we are about to engage in is no different.

Because this book is not written for the person with training in theology, and having the understanding that every person operates on a different knowledge level, I cannot assume my readers have any particular knowledge base on which to build. Therefore, the concepts covered here will become the building blocks required to aid in understanding the concepts to be presented in the following chapters. Those of you that have training in systematic theology should find most of the information in this chapter to be a review of your knowledge base.

A BRIEF DISCUSSION ON METAPHYSICS

There are many theories and questions within Epistemology, also understood as the study of the nature of knowledge, which seeks answers to questions such as, How do we know what we know? Can we truly know anything? What is real or not real, based on our knowledge? These questions eventually lead us to the ultimate question, What is reality? When this ultimate question is asked, we now enter the philosophical discipline of Metaphysics.

Metaphysics is a branch of philosophy that studies the nature of reality and tries to answer the ultimate questions concerning the nature of things, such as the nature of God, the nature of man, the nature of the universe and so on. Peter van Inwagen wrote a paper in 2007 and was published on the *Stanford Encyclopedia of Philosophy* website, which tells us that the philosophy of metaphysics could be traced back to the great philosopher Aristotle who, never using this term himself, contributed to the development of this discipline in the following manner: "He had four names for the branch of philosophy that is the subject-matter of Metaphysics: 'first philosophy,' 'first science,' 'wisdom' and 'theology.'" [1]

Ultimately, Metaphysics develops concepts from the science of physics and seeks answers to the question of the nature of things. Expressing this as a question, we would ask, What is the true nature of the existence or beginning of anything? What was the first cause of all other causes? Thus, Metaphysics is the study of the nature of things.

Within this book, I will be presenting to you biblical concepts that fall into the category of what I term "Christian Metaphysics" or "Metaphysics from a biblical perspective." To do this, there must be one presupposition assumed beforehand, and will be assumed throughout this book. That presupposition is that the Bible or the Scriptures are the inerrant and infallible words of God himself.

To expand this concept, it should be said that the Scriptures provide a means for God to reveal to the world his truth through divine revelation, and without this revelation we would have no way of knowing the facts which are revealed in them, such as the origins of humanity and the universe, the origins of the Jewish and Christian faiths, the origins of good and evil, and information explaining the personhood and nature of the creator God, along with other revelational information. This concept would also be true about you. If the history of you and your family were never revealed to anyone, then no one would ever know anything about you. The same is true for God. The

Scriptures are God's introduction to the world to who he is, and what he wants us to know about himself and his creation.

THE PURPOSE FOR PRESUPPOSITIONS

Within science, there are methods to carry out experiments and to conduct research. To help prevent duplication of facts, wasting time proving knowledge that already exists and cannot be changed, there exist presuppositions. An example of this can be found in the area of physics through the laws of thermodynamics; these laws, discovered through experiments and research, can be used as presuppositions to aid in other experiments, helping in the journey to scientific discoveries.

From the concepts discussed in the previous paragraph, we move from the physical, touchable world to the unknown, untouchable world, or to the world searching for the nature of things. What holds an atom together? We do not know. What was the first cause to the existence of the universe? From a scientific perspective, we do not know. What is life? We do not know. All of these questions deal with unseen, untouchable unknowns; these questions then become part of the world of science known as Metaphysics. Yes, I did say "science." According to Merriam-Webster's 11th Collegiate Dictionary, the first definition of science is "the state of knowing: knowledge as distinguished from ignorance or misunderstanding." [2]

Physics' first law of thermodynamics presents the concept that energy can change forms but cannot be created or destroyed. This natural law proves that within the nature of the universe, man cannot create or destroy energy. This concept also demonstrates that all energy within the universe is eternal. If this eternal concept is true, then where do we go to answer the question, where did the law of eternalness come from?

To answer that question, we must delve into some knowledge base. Since there is no physical evidence to answer that question, we must move into the realm of the philosophical world called Metaphysics, which is based on the laws of physics and its presuppositions, along with the use of human logic based on human reason.

To support this concept of using human logic and reason within theology, William Wainwright makes the following observation concerning Metaphysics as it fits into the broader branch of philosophy called "Philosophy of Religion."

> The most salient feature of this sort of philosophy of religion is its attempt to establish truth about God or the Absolute on the basis of unaided reason. Aquinas is instructive. Some truths about God can be known only with the help of revelation. Examples are his triune nature and incarnation. Other truths about him, such as his existence, simplicity, wisdom, and power, are included in his revelation to us but can also be known through reason. And Aquinas proceeds to show how reason can establish them. What we would today call philosophy of religion (or natural theology) is thus an integral part of his systematic theology.[3]

This brings us to the Bible or the Scriptures, for it is the Scriptures that provide us with God's revelation, building our knowledge base with information to the origins of life (Genesis 1), his nature, and questions that deal with the nature of things.

Throughout modern history, the Scriptures have been attacked on a historical and philosophical basis. Nevertheless, in the end, science and other historical records have supported the claims of the Scriptures. From archaeological finds, to scientific evidence, to independent historical accounts, every prophecy (which are in the hundreds) made in Scripture concerning past historical events have been fulfilled, hundreds or thousands of years after their predictions. (Many prophecies reference the first incarnation of Jesus Christ as reflected in Luke 24:44.) Within all of this, there is sufficient evidence to give the Scriptures the "right" to speak to the question of the nature of things. Thus, we will use these sixty-six books from the canonized Scriptures as the source of our knowledge base on the subject of metaphysics, in pursuit of the questions relating to the nature of things.

Because the Scriptures have made the claims of being a product of God, as well as his inspired words (2 Timothy 3:16; 2 Peter 1:21-22), I will hold to those claims and the whole of Scripture as my only presupposition. I therefore view the Scriptures, as science views the first law of thermodynamics, a proven fact that is unchangeable. Therefore, holding to the presupposition that the Scriptures are divinely inspired gives us a source that builds a credible and stable knowledge base, and a source that is researchable and applicable to this book. This is required to develop, logically and reasonably, the concepts that will be presented within these pages.

BIBLICAL HERMENEUTICS: A FOUNDATIONAL CONCEPT

Hermeneutics is the art and science of Scripture interpretation. Without proper guidelines, our interpretations could ultimately bring us to misinterpretations and thus, the wrong concepts for application. Milton S. Terry, a devoted author and student on the subject, states, "Hermeneutics properly begins, and aims to establish the principles, methods, and rules which are needful to unfold the sense of what is written. Its object is to elucidate whatever may be obscure or ill-defined, so that every reader may be able, by an intelligent process, to obtain the exact ideas intended by the author."[4] The next logical question may be, Where do we obtain these rules? The answer is, the Scriptures.

As a foundational concept in hermeneutics, it should be understood that one must possess the Spirit of God to obtain illumination or understanding to biblical truth. This concept is declared for us in First Corinthians 2:11-14, which states:

> For to us God revealed them through the Spirit; for the Spirit searches all things, even the depths of God. For who among men knows the thoughts of a man except the spirit of the man, which is in him? Even so the thoughts of God no one knows except the Spirit of God. Now we have received, not the spirit of the world, but the Spirit who is from God, that we might know the things freely given to us by God, which things we also speak, not in words taught by human wisdom, but in those taught by the Spirit, combining spiritual thoughts with spiritual words. But a natural man does not accept the things of the Spirit of God; for they are foolishness to him, and he cannot understand them, because they are spiritually appraised.

The term "hermeneutics" within Christendom carries a vast and differing understanding, both in rules and in purpose. There are those that believe there are other sources beside the Scriptures to obtain guidelines for rule making. Differing Christian groups, and groups classified as religious cults, supplement their hermeneutical rules using other books they equate equal to the Scriptures. This allows them to arrive at conclusions different from a Christian orthodox view. A non-orthodox view is one that contradicts historical teachings of Jesus Christ, the Apostles and the true prophets of God, as recorded for us in the original Scriptures. Therefore, it is necessary to give some explanation to the approach taken in this book.

As stated before, proper hermeneutics should be based on the Scriptures, sound linguistic principles, and historic background and cultural settings—not church traditions, the Apocrypha, the Book of Mormon, Seventh Day Adventists' supplemental Scriptures, Christian Science's *Science and Health with Key to the Scriptures*, Jehovah Witnesses' publication *The Watch Tower*, or any other written supplements.

Continuing our discussion, my methodology stems from two primary sources for instructions on hermeneutical principles: *Biblical Hermeneutics* by Milton S. Terry and *The Interpretation of Prophecy* by Paul Lee Tan (of which I own a signed copy). It was interesting to note the Scripture Dr. Tan listed under his signature (Colossians 3:23-24). I interpreted this passage to represent his view that his work on this topic was meant to be right, truthful, and honest before God, his ultimate critic and judge.

At this point, I want to say that my method of hermeneutical interpretation is the literal, Grammatico-Historical Method. Paul Lee Tan (Th.D) explains it this way:

> The literal method of interpreting God's Word is a true and honest method. It is based on the assumption that the words of Scripture can be trusted. It assumes that since God intends His revelation to be understood, divine revelation must be written based on regular rules of human communication.
>
> To "interpret" means to explain the original sense of a speaker or writer. To interpret "literally" means to explain the original sense of the speaker or writer according to the normal,

customary and proper usages of words and language. Literal interpretation of the Bible simply means to explain the original sense of the Bible according to the normal and customary usages of its language.

In order to determine the normal and customary usages of Bible language, it is necessary to consider the accepted rules of grammar and rhetoric, as well as the factual historical and cultural data of Bible times. Therefore, the literal method of interpretation is also called the Grammatico-Historical Method.[5]

To know more on this method of hermeneutics, pick up a copy of the authors' works I mentioned. It should be noted that the only difference in approaches to this subject, between the two authors mentioned, is in the area of prophecy.

THE CONCEPT OF TRUTH

It is sad that such a concept must be reinforced as a fundamental principle for understanding this book. Nevertheless, research has suggested that 90% of all Christendom does not believe in absolute truth, even though the Scriptures present just that concept. Another reason for this discussion is to present additional concepts to understanding the Scriptures and their structure, as well as concepts that will apply to our discussion on the nature of things.

Pontius Pilate asked Jesus Christ the question, "What is truth?" At the time, Jesus did not answer that question, but did make the following statement a few hours earlier as he prayed to his heavenly Father. "Sanctify them in the truth; Thy word is truth" (John 17:17). As the Son of God, Jesus Christ was validating what the psalmist proclaimed in the Old Testament, "The sum of Thy word is truth, and every one of Thy righteous ordinances is everlasting" (Psalm 119:160). The concept presented here is simple: The words of God and his declared principles are true. To aid us further in our understanding of what truth is, let us put meaningful boundaries on the term.

When we refer to God's Word as truth, we are referring to the truthfulness of God himself. It is important to understand that truthfulness is part of God's very nature. What does that mean? It means that God cannot lie; it is not within his character of his person or within his nature as God.

When we say that God is omnipotent, we do not mean that God is all-powerful to the point that he can do anything. It means God can do anything he chooses without anyone able to oppose him, and is only limited by his nature. Therefore, God by nature cannot lie (Proverbs 12:22, Leviticus 19:11, Titus 1:2) or break any unconditional covenants he has made with man, which would constitute a lie, or deny himself (2 Timothy 2:13); nor can God change his nature (Malachi 3:6) or be tempted by evil (James 1:13).

ADDITIONAL CONCEPTS TO BIBLICAL TRUTH

The Concept of Consistency

In like manner to God's attributes, truth has its attributes. For example, biblical truth has no contradictions. <u>For biblical truth to be true, it must agree with all other biblical truth.</u> This is a fundamental concept to this book and is why we are spending the time discussing the issue. Within these pages, the concepts presented to you will be true both in the Old Testament as well as in the New Testament. If they are not, then we have not quite reached the whole truth, and we need to continue searching and asking God to open our eyes to see it. This is the principle I applied to validate many of the concepts presented within these pages.

Progressive Revelation

One very important concept to biblical truth is that it is progressive. Although we lacked knowledge about some truth in the past, that lack of knowledge does not constitute an untruth. For example, even though mankind did not know about or understand the concept of gravity in ancient days, the law of gravity still existed and functioned all the same.

The Scriptures came to us through progressive revelation; that is, God's revelation comes to us in a progressive manner. Over time, God revealed to us his words using forty authors covering a period of about 1,500 years.

The Concept of Mysteries

Because of the nature of progressive revelation, there are truths that always existed, but were not revealed to us until later. The truth of these statements falls under the concept of "mystery" in the Scriptures.

Mysteries were persons or concepts not revealed openly and clearly to us in the Old Testament, but came to us later, by the will of God, through the writings of the New Testament (Colossians 1:26-27, Ephesians 3:1-13). Examples of this are topics such as Jesus Christ (Romans 16:25, Ephesians 5:32), the Holy Spirit (2 Thessalonians 2:7-10) and the Church (Ephesians 5:32, Romans 11:25-27), as well as the rapture or Christ's second coming, not to be confused with the Second Advent (1 Corinthians 15:51, 2 Thessalonians 2:7-10). By examining the Scriptures listed after each example, you will find the evidence supporting this assessment. Some of these passages are very clear on the matter, and others require some thought. Let us look at the more difficult passage to see if we can gain some clarity.

For the sake of context, I will reference the entire first paragraph in Second Thessalonians chapter two:

> Now we request you, brethren, with regard to the coming of our Lord Jesus Christ, and our gathering together to Him, 2 that you may not be quickly shaken from your composure or be disturbed either by a spirit or a message or a letter as if from us, to the effect that the day of the Lord has come. 3 Let no one in any way deceive you, for it will not come unless the apostasy comes first, and the man of lawlessness is revealed, the son of destruction, 4 who opposes and exalts himself above every so-called god or object of worship, so that he takes his seat in the temple of God, displaying himself as being God. 5 Do you not remember that while I was still with you, I was telling you these things? 6 And you know what restrains him now, so that in his time he may be revealed. 7 <u>For the mystery of lawlessness is already at work; only he who now restrains will do so until he is taken out of the way.</u> 8 And then that lawless one will be revealed whom the Lord will slay with the breath of His mouth and bring to an end by the appearance of

His coming; 9 that is, the one whose coming is in accord with the activity of Satan, with all power and signs and false wonders, 10 and with all the deception of wickedness for those who perish, because they did not receive the love of the truth so as to be saved. 11 And for this reason God will send upon them a deluding influence so that they might believe what is false, 12 in order that they all may be judged who did not believe the truth, but took pleasure in wickedness. (2 Thessalonians 2:1-12)

This passage is dealing with the revelation of the antichrist, as the seven-year tribulation period will begin at some point in the future, although some may interpret this passage as taking place sometime during the tribulation. The point I want to draw your attention to is underlined in this passage. The restrainer is referred to, as "he," and "he" will be removed from the scene. Who is "he"? The Holy Spirit, and if you think this through, one of the mysteries revealed to us is having Christ in you (Colossians 1:27). How do we receive or get Christ in us? Through the work of the Holy Spirit—thus, if the restrainer is removed from the world, so must we (the body of Christ) as well, because we are the temple of the Holy Spirit (1 Corinthians 6:19), adopted sons of God (Romans 8:15, Ephesians 1:5), ever sealed by the Spirit for eternity through Jesus Christ (2 Corinthians 1:22, Ephesians 4:30). This permanent sealing will be covered later in another chapter, for it too is part of understanding the nature of God and Mankind.

CLOSING COMMENTS

It is under these concepts presented thus far that I will be developing some new truths not yet understood, but will soon be explained within these pages. Whether you are skeptical of this statement or not, I trust your curiosity and thirst for knowledge will keep you reading on.

As we come to the end of this foundational chapter, and move on into the pages of this book, remember these concepts; they will serve you well as we begin exploring some complex but exciting concepts concerning God and the nature of things.

Chapter One Endnotes

———————————

[1] Peter Van Inwagen, "Metaphysics", Stanford Encyclopedia of Philosophy (Fall 2010 Edition), ed. Edward N. Zalta, 10 September 2007, [Encyclopaedia of Line]; available from http://plato.stanford.edu/archives/fall2010/entries/metaphysics/#WorMetConMet; Internet; accessed 24 August 2010.

[2] By permission. Merriam-Webster's Collegiate® Dictionary, 11th Edition©2011 By Merriam-Webster, Incorporated (www.merriam-webster.com).

[3] The Oxford Handbook of Philosophy of Religion, ed. William J. Wainwright (New York: Oxford University Press, 2005), 3-4. By permission of Oxford University Press, Inc. (www.oup.com).

[4] Milton S. Terry, Biblical Hermeneutics (Grand Rapids: Zondervan Publishing House, 1974), 19.

[5] Paul Lee Tan, The Interpretation of Prophecy (Winona Lake: Assurance Publishing, 1978), 29.

Chapter Two

THE NATURE OF GOD
SPIRIT (OT: RUWACH / NT: PNEUMA)

When we speak about the nature of things, there begins to be created a great chasm between the intellectuals of the world. It seems that when we attempt to define the term "nature," we discover that there is great disagreement on how to do so.

Since childhood, my mind has always worked toward understanding the "why" question, and to work toward making the complex simple. How is this done? We simply organize the complex into simpler forms that we can grasp, thus providing a way for understanding the nature of things. This is what scientists do every day. For example, we once understood that there is a physical object, then we came to the understanding that this object is made up of molecules, then we came to the understanding that the molecules are made up of atoms, and then we came to the understanding that atoms are made up of protons, neutrons, and electrons. We have taken the complex to the simple by understanding its foundational building blocks. However, until we understand the force or energy that holds the atom together, we have not truly understood the nature of things.

To understand an issue or someone's argument about anything, one would need to understand the very nature of the issue, which is the foundational question concerning anything. It has always been my belief that if you don't ask the right questions, you won't get the right answers.

Come explore with me the concept of the nature of things, and to be more specific, the nature of God.

THE CONCEPT OF NATURE

The great intellectuals of the world have argued the point of "what is nature" in every conceivable manner, with every contingency possible, to describe all that is covered by natural law or what is included in the understanding of the nature of the universe. In the end, scientists and philosophers have, in essence, broken down our universe into two dimensions: "natural" and "supernatural." Nature could be understood as follows: "Nature" includes everything that falls under time and space, and includes all forms of beings, which have an effect on the natural universe.

It is my suggestion that this represents the first dimension. The other dimension falls under the supernatural; this would include all things that operate outside our natural universe without influencing the universe itself. It should be noted that dimension two, for many studying in this field, does not exist. It is my view through studying the Scriptures that we live in a multidimensional universe. Mankind's starting point in understanding his universe is based on the visible and touchable world, when in reality it should start with the invisible, untouchable nature of the universe. For one to define and understand the nature of the universe, one must first understand the nature of the force behind its existence.

According to our knowledge base, the Scripture, we know that in the beginning God created everything we call the natural universe (Genesis 1:1; John 1:1-3).

Therefore, God the creator is the source of the "nature of things," the first cause of all other causes. Within this context, the question should be, What holds the atom together? Colossians 1:16-17 states: "For by Him all things were created, both in the heavens and on earth, visible and invisible, whether thrones or dominions or rulers or authorities—all things have been created by Him and for Him. And He is before all things, and in Him all things hold together." According to this statement, God created the invisible, which is the foundation of the nature of things. With respect to the question of the atom, the Scriptures state, "And in Him all things hold together." In simplest terms, the power behind the atom is the nature of God. Without God's existence, our universe would not exist. This statement is not only true because God is the first cause (Jeremiah 51:15), but because God's power is an attribute and function of his nature, as it exists and interacts with his creation; thus his very nature is holding all things together, as declared for us in Hebrews 1:1-3 and Colossians 1:16-17.

As I was searching through some Bible commentaries on this issue, I came across this interesting story in reference to Colossians 1:17.

> (v. 17) "In Him all things hold together" (NIV). A guide took a group of people through an atomic laboratory and explained how all matter was composed of rapidly moving electric particles. The tourists studied models of molecules and were amazed to learn that matter is made up primarily of space. During the question period, one visitor asked, "If this is the way matter works, what holds it all together?" For that, the guide had no answer.[1]

In Romans 1:20-21 we read: "For since the creation of the world His invisible attributes, His eternal power and divine nature, have been clearly seen, being understood through what has been made, so that they are without excuse." It is evident from this passage that creation, by design, is a product of God's nature. Accordingly, the Scriptures have declared that this fact should be obvious to us all by simply looking and examining the universe in which we live. It is also obvious that God not only revealed to us his existence through divine revelation and his creation, but also things about his existing nature, which will be our primary focus in upcoming discussions.

SOME BACKGROUND TO THE STUDY BEHIND THIS BOOK

My wife and I have been married for over 35 years. About 32 years ago, my wife had a miscarriage of our second child; at that time my wife, being upset about losing a life, asked me a question we both knew the answer to, but had no supporting evidence. "When does life begin?" It was this question, which began my biblical research to gain the biblical evidence we needed for our own confirmation. After much prayer and over 450 hours in my initial study, I found myself with information that was exciting, while at the same time, overwhelming. I knew at that time, what I saw and understood was never taught to me in Church or in Bible College, which at the time of this study I managed to make it to my senior year. As I tried to share my discovery with some college professors, there was a sense of uneasiness and a shying away. Now, after additional training and working through my discoveries, I am now, by the grace of God, ready to present to you my findings concerning, the God of the Bible, his nature, and the source of the nature of things.

THE FOUNDATIONAL QUESTION OF THE STUDY

When answering the question of when life begins, I stumbled onto the Biblical concept of the true nature of God. The key question to both subjects was, What is life? Since I knew God was the life-giver, I felt that it was reasonable to expect that God would also have the answer to my ultimate question concerning life.

I began my journey by starting with a biblical word study. As I progressed, I discovered that two words would become the building blocks and the foundational pillars to understand the nature of both God and Man. What are these two pillar words? "Soul" and "Spirit"! By defining these two words and fitting the definitions into the whole of Scripture, my understanding of the nature of God was revealed to me in a new metaphysical way.

With prayer, come walk with me through this study, and I trust you will see what I see.

DEFINING SOME TERMS

Before we begin our journey into understanding God's nature, there must be some understanding to the meaning of certain words or terminology used within our discussions.

Concept(s)

When I use the term "concept" throughout this book, I am not referring to abstract ideas of the mind. What I am referring to are truths that are organized by subject matter or issues and supported by the Scriptures through direct statements or sound reasoning (Exodus 4:11; Job 13:17-28; Isaiah 1:18; Daniel 4:34-36; 2 Timothy 3:16; Acts 17:2; Acts 18:4, 19; 1 Corinthians 10:14-17).

Personhood

My definition of personhood is as follows: It is that part of God or Mankind that reflects or demonstrates the attributes of intellect, emotion and will. This concept will be our focus in chapter three.

Metaphysical

Within the context of this book, I am referring to the reality of the existence of a being, and the ontological structure of that being that may or may not be observable through the human senses. This would include supernatural beings as well as human beings. The metaphysical makeup of a being includes a reality that is ontological and epistemological. In simpler terms, the metaphysical makeup of a being includes all the attributes that make up a being, to include its nature and personhood.

Attitude

Attitude is a state of mind that results in an action taken or an emotion displayed. Attitude, in the end, is a motivator or that which generates or reflects motives. Some examples are patience, pride, kindness, selfishness, apathy, laziness, mercy, love, forgiveness, peace and self-control. Selfishness can result in the emotion of crying or laughing. Pride can result in a number of emotions being displayed or actions being carried out. The question may be asked: "Does attitude always produce some type of action or emotion?" The answer is, "No!" Why? Because even though there is always some reason or motive for an action-taking place, motives are not always acted on. Another way to view this is that attitude is a person's motivation or motivator to do anything, even if it's just to sit and meditate. It is also possible to have more than one attitude at a time. Thus, some we act upon and others we do not. This concept will be explored and expressed in detail throughout this book.

Christian(s)

According to Acts 11:26; the disciples of Jesus Christ were first called Christians in Antioch. In Acts 26:28, King Agrippa told the Apostle Paul that he had almost persuaded him to become a Christian. If you review the context of this word as used in these passages, you will find that it is directly tied to the person and work of Jesus Christ. Therefore, Christians are those who believe that Christ is God incarnate and God's only Son. If this were truly one's position, then one would have no issues with the Gospel message, as proclaimed by Christ himself, as represented in the four Gospel books in the Scriptures. According to the Scriptures, if one denies that Jesus Christ is God or believes Jesus Christ not to be equal in nature with God the Father, then by definition that person could not be classified as a Christian (1 John 2:18-23; 4:1-3; 5:20; 2 John v7-9).

DEFINING THE CONCEPT OF GOD'S NATURE

When we speak about God's nature, What are we really talking about? Within this chapter, we will be defining God's nature and the attributes associated with it. How will we do this? We simply use our researchable knowledge base in the Scriptures, utilizing them to see through the complex to the simple. Let us start our journey of understanding through definitions.

HOW WE WILL DEFINE OUR TERMS

Normally, when we define a word, we seek the etymology or the historical root meaning of that word; then we plug it into our culture and everyday usage. This is what you see when you look up a word in the dictionary. The word is spelled with its origin given; then a list of several meanings is given, depending on what part of speech (e.g. noun, verb, adjective) is used. In many cases in the English language, there are several definitions represented for the same word.

When this type of research takes place in the Scriptures, there is an additional step taken to reach its meaning, and that is, it must be translated into our language and cultural understanding. A good example of this concept is found in *Vine's Expository Dictionary of Old Testament Words*. Let us look at some excerpts for the word "Spirit."

SPIRIT [2]

SPIRIT; BREATH

ruach OT:7307, "breath; air; strength; wind; breeze; spirit; courage; temper; Spirit." This noun has cognates in Ugaritic, Aramaic, and Arabic. The word occurs about 378 times and in all periods of biblical Hebrew.

First, this word means "breath," air for breathing, air that is being breathed. This meaning is especially evident in Jeremiah 14:6. Ruach may also represent speaking, or the breath of one's mouth: "By the word of the Lord were the heavens made; and all the host of them by the breath of his mouth" Psalm 33:6; cf. Exodus 15:8; Job 4:9; 19:17.

Second, this word can be used with emphasis on the invisible, intangible, fleeting quality of "air": "O remember that my life is wind: mine eyes shall no more see good" Job 7:7.

Third, ruach can mean "wind." In Genesis 3:8 it seems to mean the gentle, refreshing evening breeze so well known in the Near East: "And they heard the voice of the Lord God walking in the garden in the cool [literally, "breeze"] of the day..." It can mean a strong, constant wind: "...And the Lord brought an east wind upon the land all that day, and all that night..." Exodus 10:13.

Fourth, the wind represents direction. In Jeremiah 49:36 the four winds represent the four ends of the earth, which in turn represent every quarter: "And upon Elam will I bring the four winds [peoples from every quarter of the earth] from the four quarters of heaven, and will scatter them toward all those winds; and there shall be no nation whither the outcasts of Elam shall not come."

Fifth, ruach frequently represents the element of life in a man, his natural "spirit": "And all flesh died that moved upon the earth... All in whose nostrils was the breath of life..."

Genesis 7:21-22. In these verses the animals have a "spirit" (cf. Psalm 104:29). On the other hand, in Proverbs 16:2 the word appears to mean more than just the element of life; it seems to mean "soul": "All the ways of a man are clean in his own eyes; but the Lord weigheth the spirits [NASB, 'motives']." Thus, Isaiah can put nepesh, "soul," and ruach in synonymous parallelism: "With my soul have I desired thee in the night; yea, with my spirit within me will I seek thee early..." Isaiah 26:9. It is the "spirit" of a man that returns to God (Ecclesiastes 12:7).

Sixth, ruach is often used of a man's mind-set, disposition, or "temper": "Blessed is the man unto whom the Lord imputeth not iniquity, and in whose spirit there is no guile" Psalm 32:2.

Seventh, the Bible often speaks of God's "Spirit," the third person of the Trinity. This is the use of the word in its first biblical occurrence: "And the earth was without form, and void; and darkness was upon the face of the deep. And the Spirit of God moved upon the face of the waters" Genesis 1:2. Isaiah 63:10-11 and Psalm 51:12 specifically speak of the "holy or free Spirit."

Eighth, the non-material beings (angels) in heaven are sometimes called "spirits": "And there came forth a spirit, and stood before the Lord, and said, I will persuade him" 1 Kings 22:21; cf. 1 Samuel 16:14.

Ninth, the "spirit" may also be used of that which enables a man to do a particular job or that which represents the essence of a quality of man: "And Joshua the son of Nun was full of the spirit of wisdom; for Moses had laid his hands upon him..." Deuteronomy 34:9. Elisha asked Elijah for a double portion of his "spirit" (2 Kings 2:9) and received it.

As you can see, defining a term in Scripture can be very complicated. It is even suggested here that "soul" and "spirit" are used interchangeably. So how shall we proceed? Let me take you back to one of our foundational concepts, hermeneutics.

Within Milton Terry's book on hermeneutics, he made this interesting observation:

When Christianity introduced a new life and religion into the world, its sacred books were all written by Jews or Jewish proselytes, who used the later Hebraic or Hellenistic Greek. These writers found it necessary again to use this language for the setting forth of ideas and truths which has never before been clothed in any human language. New significations thus become attached to old words, and new forms of speech were coined to express the concepts of the Gospel. Accordingly, the New Testament language and diction have, necessarily, peculiarities of their own.[3]

Another way of saying this is that a new concept sometimes requires using old words or meanings and changing them to explain or express new ideas. The concept of the person of the Holy Spirit was never understood by the world until the time of Christ—thus, the need to use existing words to explain a new concept. Another example of this concept can be found in the teaching of the trinity; God was not only one, but also three. For thousands of years, the Hebrews or Jews quoted, and only understood the concept expressed in Deuteronomy 6:4, "Hear, O Israel! The Lord is our God, the Lord is one!" Jesus confirmed this teaching in Mark 12:29.

Since the days of Christ, the presentation of the Holy Spirit had become a new teaching and concept presented to us by Christ and the New Testament authors (Matthew 3:11; 12:32; 28:19; John 14:26; 1 Corinthians 6:19; Ephesians 4:30; Hebrews 10:12-17). How was this done? Through progressive revelation, the New Testament revealed additional information about the term or subject, bringing us additional meaning and understanding to the concept. This is what took place concerning Christ's teaching on the new concept of the church, as he presented to us a new mystery in the New Testament (see Matthew 16:18; Ephesians 3:1-12; Colossians 1:24-27).

Therefore, in light of this hermeneutical concept within our study, we need to redefine our understanding of the words "soul" and "spirit" in a new way that is biblical and reasonable. Let me suggest to you that we study these words through the concepts of context and usage that fits the whole of Scripture, then attach attributes or function to the words as suggested by the context as they appear in Scripture. Let us also look at how the words are used in each case as they are translated for us into the English language. **To keep things simple, let us use the King James Version of the Bible (KJV), to reference where these words are used in our English translation of the Scripture.** As a side note, within the KJV, the term "Holy Ghost" appears about 90 times in the New Testament, and is in reference to the Holy Spirit. This term uses a different Greek word then that used for the term "spirit" that we are examining in this chapter. In the KJV, there are over 220 references to the word "spirit" in the Old Testament, and in the New Testament, over 245. We will not cover the usage of these words in every case, but you can find a list of the words each time they were used, and how I defined their usage in appendices A and B.

We will start with the word "spirit" and place the word into categories that define how the word is used. As we define the categories, we will begin to see how some of these definitions fit the concept of God and his nature. What we are about to do is organize God's metaphysical makeup into parts that will help us see, and understand what makes God—God.

Because I interjected the term "parts" here, I must make a passing comment for the benefit of my scholar friends in the fields of theology and philosophy. I am fully aware of the doctrine of simplicity, and I am not advocating that somehow God is made up of physical parts or is dependent on anything. What I will be advocating is that God is spirit, singular, and that God is ontologically made up of both soul and spirit as two distinguishable functioning parts of his singular spirit essence. This will be explained in detail as we advance through this book.

Within this chapter, we will not be discussing God's personhood; this will be covered in our next chapter. As we progress with this discussion, I will translate our word study findings into visual aid drawings and build for you, in a visual way, the metaphysical makeup of God. Within subsequent chapters, the same will take place for the metaphysical makeup of man and Christ, then how all this works together as God has designed it to be.

THE CONCEPT OF SPIRIT

As seen in our Bible Dictionary example concerning "spirit," there were nine identifiable usages for that word in the Scriptures. Within my study, I took the same word and broke down its usage based on context of usage, and attached to it attributes as seen in the context in which they appear, providing the word with function. Attributes are inherent characteristics. With reference to God, they are inherent characteristics of his nature and personhood.

OLD TESTAMENT USAGE OF SPIRIT

Within the Old Testament, we can place the word "spirit" into six categories: the Holy Spirit, the spirit of God, the Spirit of the Lord, the spirit of man, the spirit of attitude and evil spirits.

Let us look more closely at the concept of "spirit" through our categories, and then apply some analyses to how this fits into our discussion of the nature of God.

The Holy Spirit

The term "Holy Spirit" is used only three times in the Old Testament (see Psalm 51:11 and Isaiah 63:10-11). In context, the term is used as a possession. In each case, it is "thy" or "his" Holy Spirit given as a gift. There is no indication that the Holy Spirit, as spoken of in these passages, is referring to personhood, but seems to be spoken of as simply a force of God to be given as a temporary gift. Because God is spirit and holy, it would be very easy to interpret this as God's spirit being given away for empowerment to perform tasks, for God is spirit, is he not? As we move to the next category, we will begin to see some very interesting facts relating to God and his nature.

The Spirit of God

This term is used in the Old Testament fourteen times. If you examine each case, the attributes associated with it are abilities to create, communicate and empower. The first usage of this term can be found in Genesis 1:2: "And the earth was without form, and void; and darkness was upon the face of the deep. And the Spirit of God moved upon the face of the waters" (KJV). I do not interpret this as the person of Holy Spirit, but the very essence of God himself. The New Testament tells us that God is spirit, singular (John 4:24). When we say that God is spirit, we are not saying that God is a spirit being, like the angels that can only be in one place at a time. What we are saying is that God is spirit like the air of our world; it exists everywhere at once. I draw this analogue from Jesus Christ's illustration found in John 3:8-12. The spirit world is compared to the wind or air of our world, and Nicodemus, an educated man of his time, could not grasp the concept, at Jesus' amazement.

You will also note that this term does not reference any personality. It does reflect power and ability, and it is what I believe to be, what I term the *nature* of God. It is that part of God that functions with power, provides communications between the trinity and any other spirit beings God created, and is that part of God that generates and reflects attitudes. God is spirit, and any attributes associated with this spirit would be defining the very metaphysical single essence of God.

Someone I had reviewing this book made the comment, "Could this be equated to the 'Force' in '*Star Wars*'?" Being an avid follower of that movie series, I instantly understood the comment. After thinking through the concept, I was surprised to find myself agreeing with the analogy, to a point—minus the "Dark Side." The "Force" in "*Star Wars*" connects and flows through everything in the universe; you just have to know how to access it for personal use. In my assessment, God's spirit or nature connects God to everything in existence for his own purposes. In either case, the attributes of both examples are similar in concept. Both exist everywhere; both provide power; both bring ability to communicate and create connectivity outside ourselves to others. Their opposites would be firstly that the Force can be used for evil, representing the "Dark Side," while the spirit of God is Holy and no evil can be contributed to it. Furthermore, The Force is impersonal, where the spirit of God is connected to a controlling personality representing deity. Consequently, my only purpose in using this analogy is to help us visualize the nature of God and how it functions in our reality of understanding. I hope this portion of our discussion has been more helpful than confusing.

Within the fourteen Old Testament references to this term, we see associated the attributes of power to create, and the ability to come and go at will. We also see the attribute of wisdom associated to understanding and knowledge (Exodus 31 and 35); we will see why this is significant later in our discussions.

Spirit of the Lord

This term is used in Scripture thirty-one times: twenty-six times in the Old Testament and five times in the New Testament. In context, it is my view that this term is in reference to the Holy Spirit, the third person of the triune God. The key Scriptures that indicate this are Second Samuel 23:2, Ezekiel 11:5 and Second Corinthians 3:17. Each of these verses refers to personhood. That is, the spirit of the Lord spoke, not just provided enablement to perform a task. The clearest indication of my assessment is found in the context of Second Corinthians 3:17, which states clearly: "Now the Lord is that Spirit: and where the Spirit of the Lord is, there is liberty" (KJV). Who is the Lord of the Bible? God is! Isaiah 42:8 states: "I am the Lord, that is My name; I will not give My glory to another, Nor My praise to graven images."

Spirit of Man

This term is used four times in Scriptures, but is referenced many times in differing manners. Examples of this can be found in Daniel 2:1, 3; Ezekiel 13:3; and First Corinthians 2:11.

The term "spirit," when in reference to man, is used to reference the life of humankind or an attitude displayed by humankind. In the end, it is my view that the spirit of man is referencing man's old nature or sinful nature, thus, the very motivator of man. It is that part of man that generates and reflects attitudes, and within mankind's fallen state, reflects the attributes of Satan's attitudes. This will be explored in more detail in following chapters.

Spirit of Attitude

Some examples of this usage are listed as follows: First Corinthians 4:21, Matthew 5:3, Isaiah 57:15, and Proverbs 16:18, 19. The theme of Attitude is big in reference to the word "spirit" within the Scriptures, and in my view and interpretation, "spirit," other than the Holy Spirit and references to him, never references personhood, which is intellect, emotion or will. This point will also be expanded in a later place in our discussion.

Evil Spirits

This term can be tricky in how one can interpret this concept. The term is used eight times in the Old Testament and twice in the New. The New Testament refers to evil spirits as "demons." However, in the Old Testament, in each case, the Scriptures state that God sent an evil spirit. How should we interpret that? Is this spirit part of God? Or, is this spirit evil, and controlled by God? Let us think through this for a moment.

To the first question, the Scriptures state the following: "For Thou art not a God who takes pleasure in wickedness; No evil dwells with Thee" (Psalm 5:4). This concept is expanded for us, as the Scriptures also state: "Beloved, do not imitate what is evil, but what is good. The one who does good is of God; the one who does evil has not seen God" (3 John 11-12). From these passages I would conclude that evil is not part of God. Therefore, this evil spirit spoken of in the Old Testament is not a spirit of God's kingdom.

To the second question, it is true that God can command evil spirits, and they obey. This was demonstrated by Jesus Christ in the New Testament as he commanded demons to exit the bodies of living souls (Matthew 5:1-13; Luke 4:41).

It is the latter that I believe to be the case concerning the usage of this term, but not to the point of human possession, as took place with Judas Iscariot (Luke 22:3), but to the point of mental influence. This concept of influence is significant and will be explored in later chapters.

NEW TESTAMENT USAGE OF SPIRIT

In the New Testament, "spirit" is referenced in the same way as in the Old Testament, with several additions. These additions are the result of Christ and the Holy Spirit coming on the scene and being presented as persons, thus, the need to reveal both as such.

Spirit of Christ

The term "spirit of Christ," as made reference to in Romans 8:9, represents God's nature in Christ, making Christ God incarnate. Romans 8:9 states: "However, you are not in the flesh but in the Spirit, if indeed the Spirit of God dwells in you. But if anyone does not have the Spirit of Christ, he does not belong to Him." The "spirit of God" and the "spirit of Christ" in this passage are equated to be one in the same. Therefore, because Christ is not the Holy Spirit, we cannot equate the "spirit of God" and the Holy Spirit as the same spirit here. The Scriptures clearly teach that Jesus Christ and the Holy Spirit are two separate persons, as we shall see later in following chapters. So what is the "spirit of Christ"? It is used synonymously with the "spirit of God" to show that Christ and God are one in the same in nature. If you do not see it this way, I encourage you to re-read the passage over and think through just what is being said. Some may ask, Can you elaborate more on this passage? Yes, I can.

Jesus teaches us in John 15 the concept that he is the vine and we are the branches. To bear fruit from this vine, you must be part of it. Jesus also teaches us in Matthew 12 the concept of good and bad fruit. If you read and think through these concepts, what Jesus is trying to teach us is that God's nature is good, and man's nature is bad (Romans 3:9-19; Ephesians 2:1-9); therefore, in order to produce that which is good, we must possess some part of God that will allow us to produce that which is good. As believers or new creatures in Christ (2 Corinthians 5:17-19), what we possess is not just the Holy Spirit, but what the Holy Spirit brings to us. And just what is that? We, through the adoption process, are grafted into the very nature of God or the spirit of God in Christ Jesus (Romans Chapter 8). For those looking for a more definitive statement to the concept that man can inherit the nature of God, let us review 2 Peter 1:4: "For by these He has granted to us His precious and magnificent promises, in order that by them you might become partakers of the divine nature, having escaped the corruption that is in the world by lust." Does this mean human beings cannot do good things if they have not been grafted into God's nature? We shall speak more on that issue in another chapter.

There are two other references that mention the "spirit of Christ" in Scripture: Philippians 1:19 and 1 Peter 1:8-11 which reads,

> And though you have not seen Him, you love Him, and though you do not see Him now, but believe in Him, you greatly rejoice with joy inexpressible and full of glory, obtaining as the outcome of your faith the salvation of your souls. As to this salvation, the prophets who prophesied of the grace that would come to you made careful search and inquiry, seeking to know what person or time the Spirit of Christ within them was indicating as He predicted the sufferings of Christ and the glories to follow.

This reference is made of God's nature, as an internal possession of the Old Testament prophets, providing them power to see into the future of the coming sufferings and glory of Christ (Isaiah 50:6, 52:13-14, 53; Acts 3:22-26, 10:43; Luke 22:44)—more evidence to what we just spoke to above.

Holy Spirit as a Person

Until the New Testament, the Holy Spirit had been seen as just that—a spirit from God that is holy and powerful. Personhood, at this point, had not been openly revealed under this term. Now, through progressive revelation of the New Testament, we begin to see something more.

Jesus begins to introduce to us a person associated with God in John 15:26. This reference is made to "another comforter" that is associated to the concept of truth, which in Scripture is only associated with God, and is personalized by the term "he," which also comes from God. If this "comforter" was an angel, it is my opinion that Jesus would have expressed it that way, perhaps using the term "angel of the Lord," as found in Genesis 16:9 or Acts 8:26. However, if we think through this concept of "comforter," we would see that this "comforter" was meant to be for all God's people everywhere. An angel cannot be everywhere at the same time. Therefore, a new concept is being presented to us, and as God's progressive revelation is revealed to us, we shall see that this other "comforter" is the person of the Holy Spirit. This becomes evident to us as we read in Romans 8:26-27: "And in the same way the Spirit also helps our weakness; for we do not know how to pray as we should, but the Spirit Himself intercedes for us with groanings too deep for words; and He who searches the hearts knows what the mind of the Spirit is, because He intercedes for the saints according to the will of God." As the Scripture begins to personalize this term as "Himself" and "He," we begin to see that this spirit is not in reference to God's essence as spirit. It is in reference to another person within God's essence, which is spirit. If you search through other Scriptures, you will find other references to the Holy Spirit, demonstrating personhood. This can be seen as the Holy Spirit exercises intellect (Mark 13:11; 1 Corinthians 2:13), emotion (Ephesians 4:30), and will (Acts 16:6).

Spirit of God as Man Possesses It

This usage is most revealing in the fact that it speaks of God's spirit or nature residing in believers or those regenerated by God (Titus 3:5). (For clarification, this spirit is not referring to the person of Holy Spirit.) Let us examine this phenomenon, for this concept leads us to a better understanding of the doctrine of adoption, and becoming a new creature in Christ. It is this concept that leads us to the understanding of our new nature in Christ vs. our old nature—the nature of Man.

In Ephesians 3:14-19 we read:

> For this reason, I bow my knees before the Father, from whom every family in heaven and on earth derives its name, that He would grant you, according to the riches of His glory, to be <u>strengthened with power through His Spirit in the inner man</u>; so that Christ may dwell in your hearts through faith; and that you, being rooted and grounded in love, may be able to comprehend with all the saints what is the breadth and length and height and depth, and to know the love of Christ which surpasses knowledge, that you may be filled up to all the fullness of God.

This is just one reference to God's spirit residing "in the inner man." We also see this concept of "abiding in" throughout the book of First John in the New Testament.

The Term "Spirit" Used by Itself

Throughout the Scriptures, the word "spirit" is used many times. Because of this, in each case you must examine its usage in context, and in most cases it will fall into one of nine categories we just spoke about. There are a few exceptions, but none that sways my interpretation from what I have just presented. Again, if in doubt as to how one would interpret the word in each case, feel free to review my interpretation in each case as seen in appendices A and B.

SUMMARY OF OUR TERMS

It has been my purpose in listing the categories for the term "spirit" that you would begin to see that the term itself does not always explain the true meaning of the word. The word can be used in many contexts and will require thought, on your part, to understand the concept of the nature of God as it is tied to the term "spirit." If your confusion is setting in, work at remembering two major concepts: first, that the Holy Spirit is a person and should not be confused with God's metaphysical makeup as spirit, or with the term "spirit of God." For God is spirit, is he not? Secondly, because the Holy Spirit is God, he also possesses the same single nature of God, which is also considered spirit. So everywhere the Holy Spirit goes, so goes the spirit of God. Let me illustrate this concept this way: Man is made up of body, soul, and spirit (First Thessalonians 5:23). Wherever you go, the body goes with you. Even though you are inside the body, you must take your body with you as you travel. So God is the same way. God is spirit; therefore, everywhere the triune personhood of God is, so is his spirit, or what I refer to as the single spirit nature of God.

I sense the frustration one might have with the phrase, "This will be discussed or explored in later chapters," but because of the complexity of these concepts, we must build knowledge in a manner as expressed in chapter one, and use a progression built through our chapters to explain the reasoning behind these concepts. Therefore, I trust you will hang in there and stay the course as we explore the many questions concerning God and the nature of things.

THE CONCEPT OF GOD'S NATURE CONTINUED

From our word categories, we must now focus on the term and concept of the "spirit of God." From this point on, I will begin to take you down a path that will reveal the attributes that are associated with the "spirit of God," or God's single essence. By doing so, we will be defining the very nature of God.

As stated before, God is spirit, and this spirit is what I believe to be the single essence and the single nature of God. How do I define nature with regard to God? God is spirit, and this spirit and all its attributes constitute the nature of God.

Understanding the Difference between God's Nature and His Personhood

Before we move forward with the concept of spirit and nature, I must emphasize at this point in our discussion that we are speaking only to God's nature and are not referring to God's personhood or Trinitarianism. It should also be noted that understanding of God's nature could also be obtained through direct statements made by God himself, or by his representatives in Scripture. An example of this can be found in Malachi 3:6: "For I, the Lord, do not change; therefore you, O sons of Jacob, are not consumed." God is declaring for himself that he does not change. Theologians call this Immutability. How do I equate this to God's nature? It is a matter of reasoning. Jeremiah 26:13 states that God will change his mind concerning a judgment pronounced, while Hebrews 7:21 states that God will not change his mind concerning his pronouncement that Christ would be priest forever. Therefore, I conclude that it is God's prerogative to change his mind anytime he chooses, with the exception of when speaking a prophecy or making an oath, unconditional promise, or unconditional covenant with himself or others (Hebrews 6:13-20); to do anything else would constitute a lie, which God states he cannot do (Numbers 23:19). It should also be noted that when God changes his mind in Scripture, it is always based on our changing behavior toward God; this is called repentance on man's part, and God's judgment changes for those that repent (2 Kings 22:15-20; Luke 13:1-5; Revelation 2:16). The changing of one's mind is directly associated with "will," which is an act of personhood. The Scriptures state that God gets angry at times (Ezra 5:12), and is pleased at other times (Luke 2:14). This is a change of emotions, which is also associated with personhood. Jesus stated that he did not know the time or the day of his return (Matthew 24:36), but he will know before his return. This is a change in his intellect, also a product of personhood. Since God cannot lie, what is God talking about when he makes the statement, "I do not change"? From reasoning through the Scriptures, it would seem logical that he is making reference to his nature, those attributes that are not related to his personhood. This statement may throw up some red flags for some, but as we press on, all will be explained to satisfy every point in our Scriptural doctrine. So the questions to be asked is, what attributes are only associated to his nature? Come; let us explore them one at a time.

THE NATURAL ATTRIBUTES OF GOD'S NATURE

What we are about to discuss is the inherent characteristics of God's nature as it is associated with God's spirit. For God is spirit, is he not? The major concept I would like to present here is that God's spirit or nature is separate in function with relationship to personhood, or that part of God that demonstrates intellect, emotion or will. As we study the Scriptures on this subject, we begin to see the relationship between nature and personhood and how they work together to make the whole essence of God. This topic of personhood and its relationship to nature will be covered in the next chapter. For now, we will be concerning ourselves with each attribute that is directly a product of God's spirit or nature.

Omnipresent

"Omnipresent" simply means that God is present everywhere; and how do we know God is omnipresent? We simply turn to our knowledge base the Scriptures. Psalm 139:7-10 states: "Where can I go from Thy Spirit? Or where can I flee from Thy presence? If I ascend to heaven, Thou art there; If I make my bed in Sheol, behold, Thou art there. If I take the wings of the dawn, If I dwell in the remotest part of the sea, Even there Thy hand will lead me, And Thy right hand will lay hold of me."

As we have pointed out before, if God's nature is holding everything together, then God's spirit also must be present everywhere, for God's spirit and his nature are one in the same. We say that God hears and sees all; this is the attribute that allows God to do this. So it is, God is present everywhere, with the ability to control all things according to his good pleasure. In the book of Exodus, God sent the ten plagues on Egypt, to include physical death. In Jonah 4:5-11, God caused a plant to grow and die overnight. In Joshua 10:12-14, God caused the Sun to stand still for about a day so that Joshua could win a battle before the Sun set. How could all this take place? It is through God's nature, which holds together and controls all things. How can God heal our bodies? It is very simple; he controls the very atoms that makeup our bodies, and if something is broken, he can simply will it to be fixed, and it is done. Does this mean God will fix everything? That's his choice. This is the concept taught to us in Romans, chapter nine. He is the potter and we are the clay. It is his choice. To some this is a comfort; to others this may be disturbing; but in the end, God's choices are always driven by his nature, which are discussed in this chapter. For the Christian, God's choices toward them are always working for their good as expressed in Romans 8:28.

Omnipotent

"Omnipotent" simply means that God is all-powerful. How should we understand this? If God is all-powerful, Can God make a rock he cannot pick up? My answer to that question goes like this; God can do anything that is not in violation of his nature or character. Examples: God cannot lie (Hebrews 6:14-16); God cannot be tempted by evil (James 1:13); God cannot deny himself (2 Timothy 2:13), and God cannot change his nature (Malachi 3:6). These are the things God cannot do. For God to create something he could not control would be a violation of his nature; for God would be denying his power and sovereignty, thus God would be denying himself—a violation of his nature.

Eternalness

God is eternal. Deuteronomy 33:27, Isaiah 9:6, Romans 16:26, Second Corinthians 4:18 and First Peter 5:10 all make reference to God's eternalness. Eternalness is part of God's nature, and our natural laws are designed around God's nature. Remember the first law of thermodynamics? Energy can change forms but cannot be created or destroyed. This is true because it is God's power flowing through his nature that maintains the atom's structure. Since God's power is eternal, so the essence of the atom becomes eternal. How should I understand this statement? The atom represents one form of energy. If we split the atom, the essence or energy of the atom's structure simply changes form to a new kind of energy. Thus, the atom's essence never really is destroyed or annihilated; it just simply changes into some other form of energy. Thus, the essence of the atom is eternal. The power behind what holds matter together is eternal, because God's nature and power is eternal. This is not the same concept as Pantheism—the idea that God and the universe are one, without personality. God lives and functions with personality and purpose, and by his will he holds all things together by the power of his nature that flows and controls all of his creation. God is not the rock or the tree, but God's nature holds the atoms together that make up the rock or the tree. This concept also refutes Gnosticism—the belief that all "matter" is evil, to include our human bodies. If God's nature is holy and perfect, and is the very power holding all things together, then by the "nature of things," matter cannot be evil—for there is no evil found in God or his nature (Psalm 5:4).

If all this is true, then what do we do with the second law of thermodynamics—the concept that all energy is in a declining state? Andrew Zimmerman Jones explains it this way:

> The second law of thermodynamics is formulated in many ways, as will be addressed shortly, but is basically a law which—unlike most other laws in physics—deals not with how to do something, but rather deals entirely with placing a restriction on what can be done.
>
> It is a law that says nature constrains us from getting certain kinds of outcomes without putting a lot of work into it,

and as such is also closely tied to the concept of the conservation of energy, much as the first law of thermodynamics is.

In practical applications, this law means that any heat engine or similar device based upon the principles of thermodynamics cannot, even in theory, be 100% efficient.[4]

It is my view that the first law is the foundational law to all other laws of thermodynamics. It is also my contention that the first law was just that—the first before the fall of man and God's curse on his creation (Genesis 3:8-24). The second law was modified by God to set limitations on nature after the fall of man and God's curse on the earth. Is this not what the Scriptures speak to when it talks about the result of God's curse, telling Adam he must work the ground all the rest of his life in toil as expressed in Genesis 3:17-19?

So how can God declare his creation eternal in light of this second scientific law? It is rather simple. The Scriptures state that God will intervene before the physical decline sees its end result (Daniel 7:13-14; Acts 3:19-26; Romans 8:21). It is a paradox; the declining state of the earth is not a decline in God's power or nature. The physical decline of our world is the result of God's curse on man and his creation over the issue of sin (Genesis 3:14-19). This curse does not affect God's nature or the concept of the first law of thermodynamics; it is only affecting the physical nature of what we see through change, not the nature of things we do not see (Psalm 78:69). By the end, God will intervene and reconcile all things to himself, and this reconciling process has already begun (Genesis 3:15; Romans 5:8-11; Colossians 1:13-20).

Allow me to illustrate the point. Psalm 104:5, Ecclesiastes 1:4 and Psalm 78:69 state that the earth is eternal. If you think through creation, everything God created may change form, but it is all still here from the beginning. We die and go back to the dust of the earth. Things rust and decay and change form, but it is still all here (Genesis 3:19; Job 34:15). Water evaporates into the atmosphere and then drops back to earth as rain, but in the end, the water is all still here, just in different states of existence. Second Corinthians 4:18 states: "While we look not at the things which are seen, but at the things which are not seen; for the things which are seen are temporal, but the things which are not seen are eternal." God's power associated with his nature is the eternal force holding all things together with personality and purpose.

Is this not what the Scriptures are talking about when they state, in Romans 1:18-20, that we should see and make the connection between God's nature and our natural universe? How awesome, the concept of God's creation.

Immutability

According to Merriam-Webster's 11th Collegiate Dictionary, the term "immutable" simply means "not capable of or susceptible to change."[5] God declares for himself that he does not change (Malachi 3:6). It is my view that this statement is in reference to his nature or what the Scriptures refer to as "the spirit of God" or "spirit," as it references any of the attributes we are discussing in this section, both natural and moral.

THE MORAL ATTRIBUTES OF GOD'S NATURE

When we speak about morality, how should we define this concept with relationship to God? Let us start by putting in context the meaning of morality as it refers to God's spirit or nature. One primary principle functioning within the nature of God is that it's within the spirit that attitude is generated and reflected. Attitude is then the controlling factor of God's personhood. Therefore, even though God is all-powerful, his power is used and controlled by his attitudes inherent to his nature. For illustration purposes, think about yourself and your ability to hurt someone. What keeps you from taking action to do so? Your attitude does. If you take on the attitude of hate, you will most likely take action to reflect your hate. If you take on the attitude of love, your action will most likely take on an action that reflects that as well. As a result, you will find the statements of the following paragraph to be true based on this concept that morality and attitude are linked together. This concept will become clearer as we evaluate God's moral attributes.

Holy

We are told by God in Leviticus 11:44-45, that we should be holy, for God himself is Holy. This attribute is the basis for all other attributes of God. *The New Unger's Bible Dictionary* expresses it this way: "(HOLINESS) Holiness is one of the essential attributes of the divine nature. It is, on the one hand, entire freedom from moral evil and, on the other, absolute moral perfection. The Scriptures lay great stress upon this attribute of God. (Exodus 15:11; 1 Samuel 2:2; Psalm 71:22; 99:9; 111:9; Isaiah 6:3; Habakkuk 1:12; Revelation 15:4; etc.)."[6]

If you study and follow this word all the way through the Scriptures, you will find it used in relationship to many things. It is referenced to God (Isaiah 6:3), places (Psalm 138:2; Revelation 21:2), people (Colossians 1:22), and things (Exodus 39:1). In light of this observation, how do I define the term "holy"? I would understand "holy" to be a standard of moral perfection, separated from all that is less than morally perfect. It could also be interpreted to mean something that is sanctified or set apart to be morally clean as opposed to morally unclean, as God defines morality. Morality is a standard of God, and can only be changed by him. What do I mean by "changed"? Acts 10:9-16 states that God declared something to be morally unclean, then changed the standard after God took action to cleanse it. Morality is totally God's standard, and his standards and conditions are revealed to us through his written word, the Scriptures (The Bible).

When we say that God is "holy," we are saying that God is morally perfect, as demonstrated through all his attributes, therefore it should be understood that all of God's attributes rest on his holiness.

SOME ATTRIBUTE EXAMPLES TIED TO HOLINESS

<u>God is Righteous</u>. (Ezra 9:15; Psalm 145:17.) This means that God is in right standing within himself as a triune God. Righteousness is directly tied to holiness. In John 17:25, Jesus addressed his heavenly Father as righteous, meaning the Father is in right standing to his holiness. Mark 6:20 makes reference to John the Baptist as being a righteous and holy man, meaning John was in right standing with God and separated from the world by God's standards. This position allowed John to act or practice right living by God's standards. John could be all this, because God's nature residing in him made him holy, just as God's nature residing in current believers puts them in the same position.

There is a great deal to be said about this concept, which will be discussed in more detail in future chapters.

God is Good. (Psalm 25:8, 119:68.) What does that really mean? The first mention of "good" in the Scripture is made in reference to God's acts—to be more specific, God's acts in the creation process. God saw that what he did was good, and said so (Genesis 1:4, 10, 12, 18, 21, 25, and 31). Therefore, anything God does is good. In Genesis 2:9, we read that God created the tree of good and evil. At this point God created man only to know and understand what is good according to God's attitudes. After man ate the fruit of this tree, as recorded in Genesis 3:5-7, man lost spiritual consciousness of God's attitudes and became conscious of new attitudes that were not good but classified as evil. What attitudes did fallen humanity take on? All that reflects Satan's attitudes: pride, lust and selfishness (Ephesians 2:3). How do we know this? In John 8:44, Jesus states: "You are of your father the devil, and you want to do the desires of your father. He was a murderer from the beginning, and does not stand in the truth, because there is no truth in him. Whenever he speaks a lie, he speaks from his own nature; for he is a liar, and the father of lies." Thus goodness, as it relates to God, is the opposite of evil. Mankind, in its fallen state, now reflects the nature of Satan through the fallen "spirit of man." Therefore, goodness is directly tied to holiness, just as righteousness is. We will continue this discussion in another chapter.

God is Merciful. (Exodus 34:6-7, KJV.) Mercy is an attitude. How do we know this? Let us reflect on Jesus' story as told to Peter in Matthew chapter 18. The key verse can be found in verse 33 as it states, "Should you not also have had mercy on your fellow slave, even as I had mercy on you?" Mercy is an attitude of forgiveness towards someone not deserving. Mercy is a derivative of God's holiness and love. This assessment is confirmed for us in Ephesians 2:4-7 and Titus 3:4-8. Thus, we can conclude that all of this collectively demonstrates that attitude is generated from, and a reflection of, God's nature.

God is all-Wise. *Merriam-Webster's 11th Collegiate Dictionary* defines wisdom this way: "a wise attitude, belief or course of action."[7] The Scriptures suggest that wisdom is a product of both the "spirit of man" and the "spirit of God." James 3:13-17 demonstrates to us that wisdom is an attitude generated from either our new nature, which is God's nature in us, or our old nature, which is our sinful nature we are born with. As you read this passage, notice the list of attitudes that are associated with the wisdom of our old nature vs. the list of attitudes associated with our new nature or God's nature in us.

> Who among you is wise and understanding? Let him show by his good behavior his deeds in the gentleness of wisdom. But if you have bitter jealousy and selfish ambition in your heart, do not be arrogant and so lie against the truth. This wisdom is not that which comes down from above, but is earthly, natural, demonic. For where jealousy and selfish ambition exist, there is disorder and every evil thing. But the wisdom from above is first pure, then peaceable, gentle, reasonable, full of mercy and good fruits, unwavering, without hypocrisy. (James 3:13-17)

As you can see through James' declaration, wisdom is also linked to God's holiness as we read the statement, "but the wisdom from above is first pure." Proverbs 3:19-20 states: "The Lord by wisdom founded the earth; By understanding He established the heavens. By His knowledge the deeps were broken up, And the skies drip with dew." If you examine closely the terms wisdom, knowledge and understanding, they are directly associated to each other. How does this relationship work? According to the Scriptures, it works like this: God's wisdom plus knowledge equals understanding. This is what Proverbs teaches us as we read in Proverbs 4:7: "The beginning of wisdom is: Acquire wisdom; And with all your acquiring, get understanding." We also see this relationship in Proverbs 2:6: "For the Lord gives wisdom; From His mouth come knowledge and understanding." In a future chapter, we will examine how this works with relationship to humans in the salvation process.

Love

God is love (1 John 4:8). Love is not an emotion, but an attitude that can generate emotion. Let us examine this concept further. In John 3:16 the word "so" in a Greek-to-English translation is "hoo'-toce," meaning "in this manner" or "thus" or "so." One could read this verse like this: for God loved, in such a manner, that he gave. Thus, love is an action stemming from an attitude. If we read the Apostle's account of what love is in First Corinthians 13, you will find a list of attitudes, not a list of emotions. First Corinthians 13:4-7 reads as follows: "Love is patient, love is kind, and is not jealous; love does not brag and is not arrogant, does not act unbecomingly; it does not seek its own, is not provoked, does not take into account a wrong suffered, does not rejoice in unrighteousness, but rejoices with the truth; bears all things, believes all things, hopes all things, endures all things." Have you ever thought of patience, kindness, jealousy, pride, selfishness, or arrogance as attitudes? Well, they are, and we will continue the discussion on this issue in a future chapter.

So when we say that God is love, what we are really saying is that God's attitude is love and is an inherent quality of God's nature. To further this concept, let us look at Galatians 5:22-24: "But the fruit of the Spirit is love, joy, peace, patience, kindness, goodness, faithfulness, gentleness, self-control; against such things there is no law." Again, this is not a list of emotions, but a list of attitudes only generated through God's nature. The person of the Holy Spirit brings to us God's nature, which gives us the ability to have such attitudes to choose from.

How does all this work with relationship to man's nature? Well, we will talk about that in the chapter that covers the nature of Man. With respect to God, attitudes are not a choice; they are inherent qualities or attributes. God is all these attitudes collectively, but with man, it becomes a choice—because of the concept of having two natures at the time we become born-again into the family of God (John 3:3-16). Through exercising our will, we must choose which nature or attitudes to follow, God's or our own. Thus, God's attitudes become ours through a new nature, which is God's; making the concept of a new and old nature residing in man look more plausible. We will explore these concepts more in another chapter.

A good example of the concept of spirit and attitude being connected can be found in Ezra 1:5: "Then the heads of fathers' households of Judah and Benjamin and the priests and the Levites arose, even everyone whose spirit God had stirred to go up and rebuild the house of the Lord which is in Jerusalem." How do I interpret this in light of all the concepts being presented here? God stirred up attitudes, which become their motivator to go, through their spirit. Attitude always generates some kind of action, either physical or emotional. An example of this concept can be seen in the emotion of anger. If our anger stems from an attitude that comes from our new nature, then anger becomes righteous, but if anger comes from an attitude of our old nature, then anger becomes sin. We are told in Ephesians 4:26 to be angry and sin not. How do we determine whether anger is sin? The answer is, by the attitude in which it is embedded. God's anger stems from his nature, which never sins; therefore, all of God's anger or wrath is always justified. However, in man, this is not always the case. In addition, this concept will be explored in more detail in future chapters.

CHAPTER SUMMARY

We have covered a great deal of ground in so little space. This may seem to be the case, because many of the concepts presented will be expanded in future chapters. However, in relationship to this chapter, allow me to review some major concepts.

One, God is spirit, singular, and it is God's spirit that metaphysically acts as his nature. The Scriptures try to give us a word picture to help us understand the metaphysical makeup of God as it illustrates for us in First Corinthians 6:16-17. God's nature or spirit is one with us if we possess it. In effect, God's attitudes become ours to choose from; thus, we can fulfill the reality of having the mind of Christ (1 Corinthians 2:16).

Second, God's nature, as we have described it here, never changes, acts as a communication path between the trinity and other spirits (1 Corinthians 2:10-11), acts as God's controlling power in the universe (Ephesians 3:16), and always reflects God's attitudes (2 Timothy 1:7). When the Scriptures refer to this spirit, it is never referring to God's personhood. This spirit is what all three persons in the Godhead share as a single entity. God only has one spirit or nature that unifies the triune personhood of God. This is why we can say that God is one. God is one in nature, and the unifying part of three persons. The personhood of God is our next topic, so come join me for chapter three.

As I stated earlier, I will now draw you a picture of this reality and build on it as we progress into the next chapter. Our discussion here is only one aspect of the only true God, the creator of all things, and the source of the nature of things.

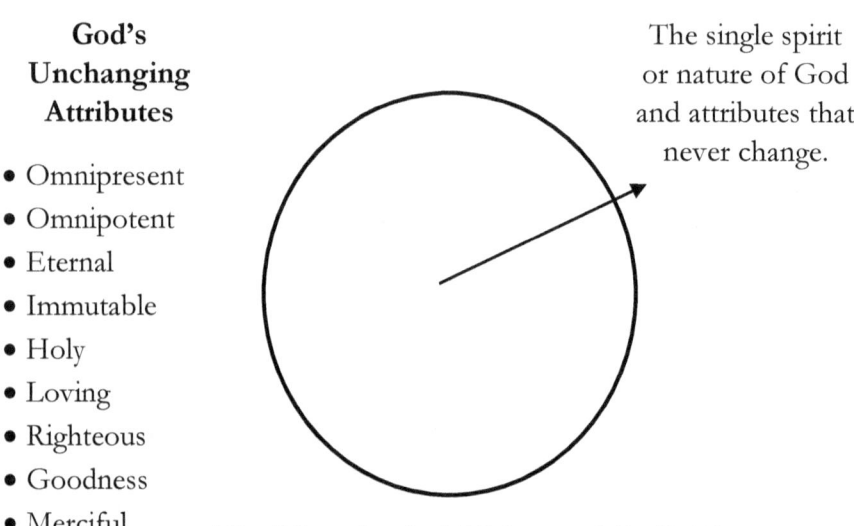

God's Unchanging Attributes

- Omnipresent
- Omnipotent
- Eternal
- Immutable
- Holy
- Loving
- Righteous
- Goodness
- Merciful
- Wisdom

The single spirit or nature of God and attributes that never change.

The Metaphysical Makeup of God's Nature
Figure 2.1

Chapter Two Endnotes

[1] Copyright 1989 Warren W. Wiersbe. The Bible Exposition Commentary: New Testament published by David C. Cook. Published permission required to reproduce. All rights reserved

[2] Vine's Expository Dictionary of Old Testament Words, s.v. "Spirit", (Nashville: Thomas Nelson Publishers Inc., 1985).

[3] Milton S. Terry, Biblical Hermeneutics (Grand Rapids: Zondervan Publishing House, 1974), 119.

[4] Andrew Zimmerman Jones, "Second Law of Thermodynamics," About.com [on line guide]; available from http://physics.about.com/od/thermodynamics/a/lawthermo_4.htm; Internet; accessed 1 March 2011.

[5] By permission. Merriam-Webster's Collegiate® Dictionary, 11th Edition ©2011 By Merriam- Webster, Incorporated (www.merriam-webster.com).

[6] The New Unger's Bible Dictionary, s.v. "Holiness", (Chicago: Moody Bible Institute, 1988).

[7] By permission. Merriam-Webster's Collegiate® Dictionary, 11th Edition ©2011 By Merriam- Webster, Incorporated (www.merriam-webster.com).

Chapter Three

THE PERSONHOOD OF GOD
SOUL (OT: NEPHESH / NT: PSUCHE)

Our study will now focus on the term "soul," and how it is used throughout Scripture. We will follow the same philosophy as in the last chapter and will not be discussing how this term is used each time it appears in both the Old and New Testaments. But, for your convenience, I will make available appendices C and D, which will list all the times "soul" can be found in Scripture, as translated into the English language, as it appears in the KJV Bible, and how I view its usage in each case. Unlike the word "spirit," the term "soul" is used in a very consistent manner.

A BIBLICAL PERSPECTIVE ON PERSONHOOD

When we begin to talk about the personhood of God within the theological community, a great debate takes place as to what that really means. Why? Because very few have challenged the fact that "soul" and "spirit" do not represent the same function as it relates to God. Yet the Scriptures have a different opinion.

As an example, First Thessalonians 5:23 states, "And the very God of peace sanctify you wholly; and I pray God your whole spirit and soul and body be preserved blameless unto the coming of our Lord Jesus Christ" (KJV). Let us break this verse down in context to the whole of Scripture for better understanding. The Apostle Paul is giving exhortation to believers in how to conduct themselves in light of the world they live in. When we get to verse 23, Paul is praying that God would sanctify them as a whole being, for the purpose of enablement to perform all that he was trying to instruct them to do. As you can see, Paul defines the whole being of man as made up of spirit, soul, and body. This prayer request only makes sense if we understand that each part of a human being has individual and important functions that work together to make the whole human being, as God has designed it. Let us break this concept down for better understanding.

The term "spirit" as we have defined it for God, is also true about mankind. As spirit functions as God's nature, spirit also functions in the same way for man—that is, the "spirit of man" acts as his old nature and is the controlling influence with relationship to attitudes. This will be examined in more detail in another chapter. Why does Paul pray to sanctify the spirit? Because the Scriptures teach in Romans 12:1, 2 that we are to present our bodies as a living sacrifice to God. Within the context of chapter 12, the body represents our whole being. Then in verse two, we read that we should be renewing our minds, for the purpose of nonconformity to the world, taking on the appropriate attitude in our thinking. This can only be done if we sanctify our attitudes; for it is attitude that controls our thinking and is a product of our spirit or nature. Sanctifying our body makes sense, because the Scriptures also teach us to take care of our physical bodies, because they do not belong to us, but to God (1 Corinthians 6:18-19)! Now let us turn to the third part that Paul made reference to, our soul. It is in our soul that we find the meaning of personhood—that part of us that functions with intellect, emotion and will. In retrospect, Paul's prayer is for us to be sanctified in our attitudes and motives (spirit), in our intellect, emotions and will (soul), and in our body, which is the temple of the Holy Spirit and the means to communicate and move about in the world in which we live. In this light, the following paragraphs, hopefully, will become a little clearer for understanding the nature of things.

To help narrow this concept down as it relates to God let us look more closely at the concepts of "soul" and "spirit." The Scriptures state in Hebrews 4:12, "For the word of God is living and active and sharper than any two-edged sword, and piercing as far as the division of soul and spirit, of both joints and marrow, and able to judge the thoughts and intentions of the heart." If we look closely at this verse, we can determine three very important concepts. First, there is a clear distinction between "soul" and "spirit," because this Scripture speaks to the fact that it can influence each of these parts individually. Secondly, the Scriptures state that they can speak to the innermost part of man, which are his thoughts and intentions. Three, if we examine this verse closely, it actually defines for us the functions of both soul and spirit. Soul produces thought, which is our intellect, and spirit produces intent or our intentions, which are our motives. This interpretation seems to bring us back to the concept that motives are generated by our attitudes. Allow me to illustrate this concept this way: If I display an attitude of selfishness, I may withhold from someone the use of something that belongs to me. My motive for doing so is selfishness. It seems that motive and attitude can be one in the same thing.

With all that has been said here, I believe we have established some credibility that "soul" and "spirit" are two separate functioning parts of our being and require additional scrutiny.

A CLOSER LOOK AT THE CONCEPT OF PERSONHOOD OF GOD

As we examine the term "soul" throughout the Scriptures, we will find that in both the New and Old Testaments, this term is used very consistently. Whenever the term "soul" is referenced in Scripture, it will 99% of the time fall into the concept of personhood, and many times will display the attributes of intellect, emotion or will. At the same time, "spirit" will 99% of the time not be associated with these types of attributes. The reason why understanding this has been so elusive is because both terms are sometimes used to represent the whole human being. But if we define "personhood" as that part of us that demonstrates the functions of intellect, emotion and will, we will begin to see that "soul" really does have a different function than spirit. Let us look at a few examples.

Intellect

We read in Psalm 13:2, "How long shall I take counsel in my soul, having sorrow in my heart daily? How long shall mine enemy be exalted over me?" (KJV) To take counsel is an intellectual exercise.

Luke 12:19 states, "And I will say to my soul, Soul, thou hast much goods laid up for many years; take thine ease, eat, drink, and be merry" (KJV). This is a demonstration of holding an intellectual conversation with oneself.

Emotion

Psalm 6:3 states, "And my soul is greatly dismayed; But Thou, O Lord—how long?" (KJV) To be dismayed according to the dictionary is to lose courage through the emotion of fear.

Jeremiah 4:19 states, "My soul, my soul! I am in anguish! Oh, my heart! My heart is pounding in me; I cannot be silent, Because you have heard, O my soul, The sound of the trumpet, The alarm of war" (KJV). Here we see the soul is in anguish, another emotion.

Will

Job 7:15 states, "So that my soul chooseth strangling, and death rather than my life" (KJV). Making a choice is an act of the will.

Psalm 33:20 states, "Our soul waiteth for the Lord: he is our help and our shield" (KJV). Waiting for something is also an act of the will.

Throughout the Scriptures, the word "soul" is used as a general reference to personhood. If you look closely, you can see that the functions attached to it are intellect, emotion and will. There are those cases where attitude may be associated, but this is because attitude is the generator of emotions. And because of this close relationship, we sometimes see them as synonymous. Let see if I can make this point a little clearer.

All emotions are a result of some type of attitude. Why are we crying? Is it because we are happy for someone (Selfless Attitude)? Or because we are mad we did not get our own way (Selfish Attitude)? Because our "soul" and "spirit" work together as a whole, these terms are sometimes interchanged in the Scriptures representing the whole person, leading us to the idea that "soul" and "spirit" are one and the same. But in reality, they are two separate parts that make up God and Mankind.

In this chapter, we want to focus on "soul" as it relates to God.

SOULSHIP AS IT RELATES TO GOD

"Soulship" is a new term I coined to express a new concept and is closely related to the concept of ownership. This was necessary at the time of writing the first edition of this book, because I could not find this word or a definition for this term when performing a word search in over 1,000 on-line English dictionaries. At the time of writing this revised edition, I have found one on-line dictionary at (oxforddictionaries.com) that has listed a definition for Soulship to mean: "The condition or state of being a soul; soulful quality." Allow me to maintain my original definition and define this term for its intended use in this book. "Soulship" should be understood to mean that the soul is metaphysically the principal owner of personhood. In using this term, what I am saying to you is that without the possession of a soul, you cannot be a person. This statement may seem reasonable to you, but when we apply this concept to God, there is a big problem. The theological community does not recognize the concept of soulship with reference to God. The concept of soulship is not just unrecognized, but also not understood conceptually by the theological community. Why? Well, let's talk about that.

Some Reasoning on Soulship

Because the terms "soul" and "spirit" have been considered interchangeable all these years, the soul has been made to reference only persons that are human beings. In reference to the Scriptures, God created a living soul in Genesis 2:7, and since God is spirit, the two terms, in reference to God, never seem to come together. Another problem has been the person of Jesus Christ being both God and Man; if this has not confused the issue, I don't know what would—thus, the purpose of this book. Within this chapter and those that follow, I will tackle these issues and clear up the confusion surrounding how Jesus can be both God and Man, and the issue of unity within the trinity, among other things. The key concept to these issues can be seen in the title of this book, *Made in the Image of God*. But for now, let's get back to soulship and how that works within this chapter.

THE PERSONHOOD OF GOD

When we speak about personhood, we generally do not relate this term to God because of the issue of soulship. All Christian theologians do recognize that God is three persons, to reflect the existence of the trinity of the Father, Son, and Holy Spirit, but may lack the understanding of how all that works together. It is also recognized by theologians that these three persons of the trinity are not the same, but just how they relate to each other in co-existence is a mystery. What we are about to do is develop a new model to help bring clarity to these issues and bring better understanding of the triune Godhead by using our researchable knowledge base, the Scriptures. How shall we start? Let us start by using our definition of "soul" and see if it fits into the Scriptures in reference to the Godhead, a theological term used to represent a triune God.

The purpose of this chapter is to establish the fact that within the Godhead or trinity, personhood lies with the concept of soul. To do this, we must look at each person of the trinity and establish soulship. In a future chapter, we will look at how this plays out with reference to Jesus Christ; thus, the length of our discussion may vary with each person of the trinity within this chapter.

Soul as It Relates to God the Father

Within the debate of soulship, what many fail to see is the ten references God the Father makes to his own soul: Leviticus 26:11, 30; Judges 10:16; Psalm 11:5; Jeremiah 5:9, 29; 6:8; 9:9; Matthew 12:18; and Hebrews 10:38. Many of these passages have reference to God displaying emotion, stemming from an attitude. Additionally, as you read these verses, you will see that God is not pleased with the situation at hand in the Old Testament, but in the New Testament, we find that God is pleased with his Son.

Because "soul" has always been considered interchangeable with "spirit," the theological community has not taken notice of these references as anything significant. But as we move to the next person in the trinity, the argument for soulship becomes more plausible.

Soul as It Relates to God the Son (Jesus Christ)

With relationship to the soulship of Jesus Christ, we find that Jesus' soul is referenced five times: Matthew 26:38; Mark 14:34; John 12:27; Acts 2:27 and Acts 2:31, with the gospel accounts referencing Jesus showing emotion and the Acts accounts referencing Old Testament prophecies tying Jesus' soul to personhood.

Why is this missed? Because somehow we just see this as part of Jesus' humanity. However, if we reason this out, there is another answer. Stay close and follow my line of thought. The Christian church has always held historically to Christ being one person and having two natures. If Christ is a person before his incarnation, then is he not the same person after his incarnation? The theological community holds that Jesus' soul was equivalent to Jesus' humanity. It is my view that the person of Jesus Christ is founded on his Soulship, and the soul that Jesus possessed was in fact his own soul as deity before his incarnation. The two natures that Christ possessed were represented by the "spirit of God" and the "sinless spirit of man," which was a result from the virgin birth (Luke 1:26-35). Christ had one soul and two spirits representing two natures. This scenario fits the whole of Scripture and will be further explored in another chapter.

Soul as It Relates to the God the Holy Spirit

Up front, I will tell you that "soul" is never mentioned with reference to the Holy Spirit. So how do we know he has one? In addition, why do you think it is never mentioned? To answer our first question, if we define personhood as Soulship, then the Holy Spirit, as a person, must have a soul. All <u>Christian</u> theologians believe that the Holy Spirit is a person; we just don't all agree to how we define that. Thus, again, the purpose of this book—to help define and reveal, in a new light, the concept of a triune God and his image embedded, by design, in mankind.

To answer the second question, my line of reasoning follows: the Holy Spirit has always acted as the silent partner of the Godhead. That is, the Holy Spirit never mentions or speaks of himself. Therefore, if one never talks about themselves or their personhood, and personhood is defined to mean soulship, then the term "soul" would never be used in reference to that person. The only thing we need to prove in Scripture is the fact that the Holy Spirit has his own intellect, emotion, and will, and always acts in the background in accordance to the other two members of the Godhead, thus never making reference to self.

We know from Scripture that the Holy Spirit was hidden throughout the Old Testament, thus always working in the background. Then, in the New Testament, we find the Holy Spirit revealed to us with some additional insights. Let us look at those for a moment. We find, in John 14:16-17, Jesus introducing us to the Holy Spirit as another Helper from God. The Scriptures state, "And I will ask the Father, and He will give you another Helper, that He may be with you forever; that is the Spirit of truth, whom the world cannot receive, because it does not behold Him or know Him, but you know Him because He abides with you, and will be in you." It is from this introduction that we begin to learn the Holy Spirit's purpose as Jesus reveals this to us in John 15:26, which reads: "When the Helper comes, whom I will send to you from the Father, that is the Spirit of truth, who proceeds from the Father, He will bear witness of Me." The Holy Spirit's primary purpose is to bear witness to the fact that Jesus is God incarnate. Later we learn that the Holy Spirit will also perform other functions in enhancing our lives and the worlds, all by being obedient to the Father and the Son. How do we know that? John 16:13-16 states, "But when He, the Spirit of truth, comes, He will guide you into all the truth; for He will not speak on His own initiative, but whatever He hears, He will speak; and He will disclose to you what is to come. He shall glorify Me; for He shall take of Mine, and shall disclose it to you. All things that the Father has are Mine; therefore I said, that He takes of Mine, and will disclose it to you." Jesus is saying that the Holy Spirit takes his direction from God the Father and God the Son. There is a great deal more the Holy Spirit does, but the point has been made to all that is required here.

SUMMARY ON THIS CHAPTER'S DISCUSSION UP TO THIS POINT

The major concept of this chapter is that personhood lies with soulship, that is, a person is a person because they possess a soul. This is true both for God and for Mankind. It has been demonstrated within this chapter that the "soul" possesses all the functions of intellect, emotion and will. It was demonstrated in the last chapter that the "spirit" acts as God's nature. Soul and spirit work together forming a single entity. At this point a visual aid may be required to see how all this works together.

Within the following diagram, I have developed figure 3.1. As you review this diagram, you will have many questions. Questions like, if personhood means soulship and a soul has intellect, emotion and will, does that mean God has three sets of intellect, emotion and will? The answer to that observation is yes! Allow me to elaborate on this truth in our next section.

72 | *THE PERSONHOOD OF GOD*

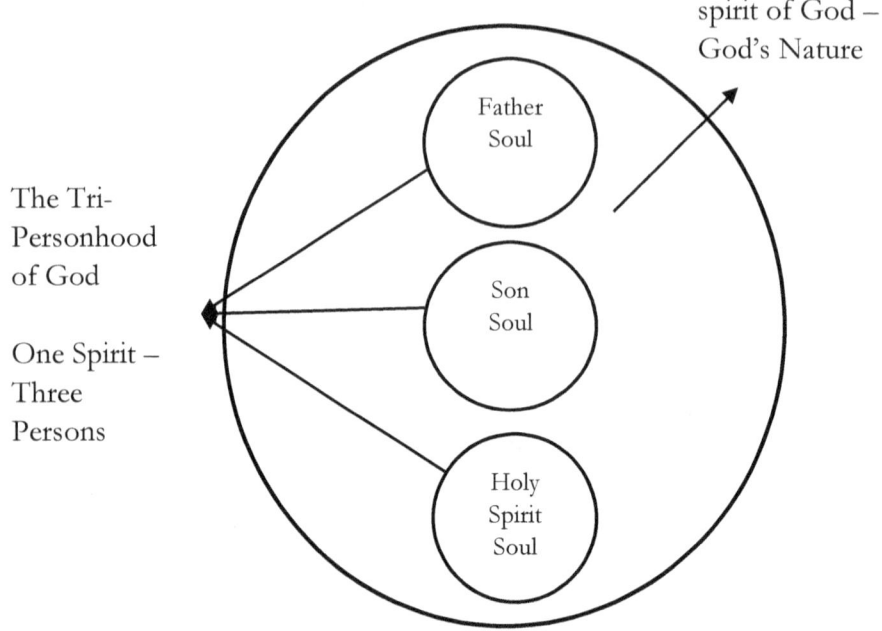

The Metaphysical Makeup of the Triune God
Figure 3.1

THE TRINITY AND THEIR RELATIONSHIP TO ONE ANOTHER

Is it possible that within the single nature of God, there are three sets of intellect, emotion and will? Well, if soulship is the principal owning concept of personhood, then this should be the reality. But is this what the Scriptures reveal to us? Let us continue our study and find out.

God the Father

It has already been established that God the Father spoke of his own soul. In the following passage, we will see the attributes that are equated to God's soul. Numbers 12:1-9 states:

> Then Miriam and Aaron spoke against Moses because of the Cushite woman whom he had married (for he had married

a Cushite woman); and they said, "Has the Lord indeed spoken only through Moses? Has He not spoken through us as well?" And the Lord heard it. (Now the man Moses was very humble, more than any man who was on the face of the earth.) And suddenly the Lord said to Moses and Aaron and to Miriam, "You three come out to the tent of meeting." So the three of them came out. Then the Lord came down in a pillar of cloud and stood at the doorway of the tent, and He called Aaron and Miriam. When they had both come forward, He said,

"Hear now My words: If there is a prophet among you, I, the Lord, shall make Myself known to him in a vision. I shall speak with him in a dream. Not so, with My servant Moses. He is faithful in all My household; with him I speak mouth to mouth, even openly, and not in dark sayings, and he beholds the form of the Lord. Why then were you not afraid to speak against My servant, against Moses?" So the anger of the Lord burned against them and He departed.

What we see here is a display of the Father's intellect (the holding of a conversation), emotion (the anger of the Lord burned), and will ("I, the Lord, shall make Myself known"). This is no surprise, but what may surprise you is what we see in relationship to the Son.

God the Son

It has already been established that Jesus has a soul. But, is it part of his humanity, or part of his deity? Luke 22:39-46 states the following:

And He came out and proceeded as was His custom to the Mount of Olives; and the disciples also followed Him. And when He arrived at the place, He said to them, "Pray that you may not enter into temptation." And He withdrew from them about a stone's throw, and He knelt down and began to pray, saying, "Father, if Thou art willing, remove this cup from Me; yet not My will, but Thine be done." Now an angel from heaven appeared to Him, strengthening Him. And being in agony He was praying very fervently; and His sweat became like drops of blood, falling down upon the ground. And when He rose from prayer, He came to the disciples and found them sleeping from sorrow, and said to them, "Why are you sleeping? Rise and pray that you may not enter into temptation."

Within this small passage we see demonstrated Christ's intellect ("Pray that you may not enter into temptation"), emotion ("And being in agony"), and will ("Father, if Thou art willing, remove this cup from Me; yet not My will, but Thine be done"). Historically the Christian church has always held that Jesus is a single person with two natures, as documented through the Nicene Creed of 325 A.D. If we can tie personhood to soulship, then in the end, Jesus as God has a soul, which would confirm what the Christian church has historically held to for nearly 2,000 years: that Jesus Christ represents both God and Man as a single person who possesses two natures. The real issue here is how these two natures are represented or defined. We will talk more on this issue in another chapter.

God the Holy Spirit

Once again, when dealing with the person of the Holy Spirit, it becomes more difficult to demonstrate personhood and the concept of soulship. This is true because of our previous discussion that the Holy Spirit never refers to himself because of the total submission of himself to the Father and the Son; thus, proving the concept of "will" becomes more difficult for similar reasons. But by reasoning through these issues, I believe we can prove the Holy Spirit has an individual "will."

Acts 16:6 states, "And they passed through the Phrygian and Galatian region, having been forbidden by the Holy Spirit to speak the word in Asia." As we can see here, it was the Holy Spirit that forbade something to take place; this is an act of the will. Acts 13:4 states, "So, being sent out by the Holy Spirit, they went down to Seleucia and from there they sailed to Cyprus." To send someone somewhere requires an act of the will.

We find in Acts 15:28, "For it seemed good to the Holy Spirit and to us to lay upon you no greater burden than these essentials:" Here we see the Holy Spirit with personal reasoning skills, reasoning over what is a good or bad idea, demonstrating intellect. Then in Ephesians 4:30 we see emotion demonstrated as we read, "And do not grieve the Holy Spirit of God, by whom you were sealed for the day of redemption."

Summary of this Section

As just reviewed, we can see through Scripture that within the Godhead there are in fact three sets of intellect, emotion, and will. Because of the many implications in other areas of theology, which can be affected by this concept, we will need to explore in more detail the concept of the trinity. As we move into chapter four, we will explore how they can all be unified within the Godhead. But first, we need to explore an additional issue with relationship to a triune God.

THE TRINITY AND THEIR RELATIONSHIP TO THEIR CREATION

Within chapter two, we talked about the omnipresence of God—the concept that God is present everywhere. If you remember, it is God's spirit or nature that allows the triune Godhead to see, hear, and communicate spirit-to-spirit to his creation, among other things. We see this many times in Scriptures by simple statements the triune God has made. Some examples can be found in Genesis 21:16-20; Exodus 2:24; Numbers 12:2; Second Chronicles 30:20; Psalm 34:6; Genesis 6:5; Exodus 3:4; 2 Chronicles 12:7 and John 1:48-50. These examples demonstrate that God the Father and God the Son both could see and hear through omnipresence. How could both do this? As Jesus stated, "My Father and I are one." Jesus and the Father share the same nature as we spoke of in chapter two. This leaves us with the issue of soulship and how it works with relationship to God's nature, and more specifically with the attribute of being omnipresent. Come join me in our last section to this chapter, as we explore more closely these issues.

OMNIPRESENCE EXPLORED

As we demonstrated in chapter two, omnipresence is an attribute of God's nature or spirit, not God's personhood. If you do not remember the difference, please review this concept in chapter two starting at the sub-title "*Understanding the Difference between God's Nature and His Personhood.*" It is my contention that God's personhood can function on a limited omnipresent basis. Before you protest this statement, allow me to clarify that I am not saying that God as a whole is not omnipresent. What I am saying is that God's personhood has the ability to limit its omnipresent attribute as God sees fit. Let us review some Scriptures that seem to reflect this observation.

Patterns of God the Father

We read in Second Samuel, chapter seven, the account of God the Father living and dwelling in tents as he traveled with his people, the nation of Israel. We see in Numbers 12:1-9 the account of God the Father coming in a pillar of cloud and standing in the door, then the statement in verse nine that God departed. These are some examples of God the Father's personhood coming and going at will.

The question maybe asked, Where is God the Father now as a person? The answer to that question comes from Jesus himself as he states in John 14:2-3: "In My Father's house are many dwelling places; if it were not so, I would have told you; for I go to prepare a place for you. And if I go and prepare a place for you, I will come again, and receive you to Myself; that where I am, there you may be also." This tells us that God the Father as a person is in a particular place. God had a conversation with Satan in Job chapter one, and asked him, where have you come from? The answer was, from earth. This tells us that wherever God the Father as a person was, it was not on earth. We are told in First Kings 8:30 that heaven is God's dwelling place. The Scriptures tells us that there are three levels of heaven. The first is a place where the earth's atmosphere exists, or what the Scriptures call the firmament; outer space consisting of the stars and planets is the second, and the place where God resides is third. How do we know there is a third heaven? The Apostle Paul speaks of it in Second Corinthians 12:2. In conclusion, as we search the Scriptures for examples of God the Father's personhood, we discover that his personhood is never represented as being omnipresent.

Patterns of God the Son

As we review God the Son's personhood, we discover that he is never presented as being in more than one place at a time, in bodily form, while on earth. But after the resurrection of Christ, we are told in Matthew 18:20 that Christ can be in more than one place, as a person, in spirit form.

We see Jesus praying in John chapter 17, demonstrating that God the Father is not present on the earth with him. Some would say this separation is only true because Jesus is in a human body; that is a reasonable assumption and to some extent true. The human body, as part of human nature, is limited. The Scriptures tell us that Jesus was limited as God while on earth (Psalm 8:4-8; Hebrews 2:6-10). But what do we do with the risen Lord in Acts 1:1-6? We are told that Jesus will return just as he left in a glorified body, coming and going from one place to another as a single person. We are also told in Revelation 19:6-16 that Christ will return a second time, just before the millennial kingdom begins, as a single person. Just like the Father, the Son is represented as being in one place at a time as a person, with one exception as spoken of in Matthew 18. So where is Christ now? The Scriptures tell us that he sits at the right hand of the Father in heaven (Acts 2:32-36; 7:56; Romans 8:34; 1 Peter 3:18-22). We will speak more on Christ in another chapter.

Patterns of God the Holy Spirit

We read in First Corinthians 6:19: "Or do you not know that your body is a temple of the Holy Spirit who is in you, whom you have from God, and that you are not your own?" From the Scriptures, we see that the Holy Spirit of God, as a person, acts and operates in a limited omnipresent mode. We also are told the same thing in Second Timothy 1:14: "Guard, through the Holy Spirit who dwells in us, the treasure which has been entrusted to you." The person of the Holy Spirit dwells with and in us collectively as believers in Christ Jesus, forming the single body of Christ, the church of the living God (Colossians 1:18-29). If the Holy Spirit is only living in those that are adopted into the family of God, then technically speaking the Holy Spirit is limiting his presence. This is not to say he is not working in other places throughout the world, but only to say, not all individuals are the temple of the Holy Spirit, leaving him working in a limited omnipresent fashion as a person.

SUMMARY OF THIS SECTION

Ultimately, we see that the personhood of God can, but does not always, act in an omnipresent manner. This is a mystery that may never be understood until heaven becomes our permanent home.

By examining this issue of the personhood of God, it is not my intent to limit God or his omnipresent attribute. God's nature or spirit as explained in chapter two is omnipresent. But his personhood in function may not always be. However you want to understand this point, it cannot be denied that this explanation of God does fit the whole of Scriptures without contradiction of God as a single entity.

As stated earlier, we can see through Scripture that within the Godhead there are in fact three sets of intellect, emotion, and will, and the attribute of omnipresence seems to function differently with relationship to his spirit or nature. Because of the many implications in other areas of theology that can be affected by these concepts, we will need to explore in more detail the concept of the trinity, and how the three persons of the Godhead are all unified. So come join me for chapter four, and let us explore the unity of God.

Chapter Four

THE UNITY OF GOD
THE TRINITY (THREE IN ONE)

Because of the subject matter covered in our previous chapters, there is required a discussion on the subject of unity within the Godhead. For without this discussion, we will be left with the concept of God in chaos. It is unity within the Godhead that maintains order in our universe and with God himself.

As part of the discussion on unity, we must revisit the problem of the concept of soulship—the idea that forces us to think of God in human terms. To recognize God as having three sets of intellect, emotion and will is a bit much to grasp. To help us contemplate this concept, let us anatomize the issue into something more manageable. When we think of humans, we can understand the concept of soulship because we know and live with all the elements that make up our personhood. We understand intellect, emotion and will. We also understand that when there is more than one person in a room, problems begin to manifest themselves. No two people have the same likes and dislikes, and there are the standard conflicts over, "I want what he or she wants." How does it all work with God? Well, let us explore that question.

THE UNITY OF INTELLECT

We will first start with the concept of intellect or having knowledge. This issue is the trickiest within the concepts being presented here because of the issue associated with an omniscient God. For centuries, God being all-knowing has been seen and understood to reference God's knowledge collectively—therefore, all three persons within the Godhead are all-knowing. If they are not, how can they all be God? These are all far-reaching assumptions that need addressing.

If you remember in Chapter Two I stated that what makes God, God is his nature. All persons who are metaphysically structured within this nature are God. Allow me to direct you back to figure 3.1. Every person that is drawn inside the circle labeled "spirit of God" is God. God is one nature or spirit, and three persons unified by that nature. This is why man can never be God. We are not metaphysically structured in the exact same way as God. Allow me to illustrate it this way: A human can never be an animal because humans are designed in a different metaphysical structure by nature. This is why I oppose the concept that humans belong in the animal kingdom, which we are taught since our elementary school days. We are not animals! We are humans created in the image of God, with the ability to know the difference between good and evil, putting us in our own kingdom, scientifically speaking. The same is true about animals, birds and fish. These creatures are all metaphysically structured differently by nature and do not reason on the same moral plane as humans. This is true because of the way God designed the nature of things, as stated in Genesis chapters one and two. Let us go back to our knowledge base, the Scriptures, to see just what God said concerning this issue. Genesis 1:24-27 states:

> Then God said, "Let the earth bring forth living creatures after their kind: cattle and creeping things and beasts of the earth after their kind"; and it was so. And God made the beasts of the earth after their kind, and the cattle after their kind, and everything that creeps on the ground after its kind; and God saw that it was good. Then God said, "Let Us make man in Our image, according to Our likeness; and let them rule over the fish of the sea and over the birds of the sky and over the

cattle and over all the earth, and over every creeping thing that creeps on the earth." And God created man in His own image, in the image of God He created him; male and female He created them.

It is evident in this passage that God created creatures after their own "kind." In today's science, "kinds" have been organized and structured into kingdoms such as the animal kingdom, the mineral kingdom, the plant kingdom and so on. Man was not made of the same "kind" as animals, but God specifically said, we (the trinity) will make man in our image and after the fall of mankind, knowing the difference between good and evil. Animals are amoral creatures and therefore different from humans. The true meaning of this statement will be explored in another chapter.

The Concept of Omniscience

With all that has been said so far, omniscience is not a product of God's nature as illustrated in chapter two, but rather an attribute of God's personhood as described in chapter three. If we follow this line of reasoning, then God, being three persons, naturally possesses three knowledge bases or intellects. How does this work within the Godhead, and does it create any problems? Well, let us see what the triune Godhead says about this issue.

God the Father's Intellect

We have talked about God the Father being the mastermind behind creation. God the Father is all-knowing because he is the author of all things. It would stand to reason that if you made all the building blocks of the universe out of nothing, that this act would also make you the author of all scientific laws that govern those building blocks. Therefore, by being the author of all created things, you would also be all-knowing concerning the nature of things. God declares for himself, through the writings of David, "Great is our Lord, and abundant in strength; His understanding is infinite." (Psalm 147:5) God not only understands all things created, but also, God understands all things concerning himself (1 Corinthians 2:10-16). Contrast this with the Scripture that speaks to the human condition as found in Jeremiah 17:9: "The heart is deceitful above all things, and desperately wicked: who can know it?" (KJV). The Apostle John writes for us in First John 3:19-20: "We shall know by this that we are of the truth, and shall assure our heart before Him, in whatever our heart condemns us; for God is greater than our heart, and knows all things." It should also be noted that God the Father is the only person of the trinity that makes the claim of being all-knowing. In contrast to God the Father's knowledge base, let us examine what Jesus says about himself with regard to this issue.

The Intellect of God the Son

Jesus gives us insight to the source of his knowledge base, as he states in John 8:27-29: "They did not realize that He had been speaking to them about the Father. Jesus therefore said, 'When you lift up the Son of Man, then you will know that I am He, and I do nothing on My own initiative, but I speak these things as the Father taught Me.'" Is this Jesus the man talking, or is it Jesus as God talking? The answer to that question may be found in John 17:5, as Jesus is praying to his heavenly Father: "And now, glorify Thou Me together with Thyself, Father, with the glory which I had with Thee before the world was." The person that Jesus was here on earth is also the same person before the creation of the universe. Our confusion comes when trying to understand the dual role of the God-Man that Jesus took on through the virgin birth.

Some would argue that when Jesus took on the form of a man, the Scriptures state he was limited; therefore as part of this limitation, Jesus' knowledge base was affected. Let us evaluate that argument.

During Jesus' ministry on earth, he demonstrated the power to know things without any input from outside sources. Example: He knew Lazarus was dead, days before he arrived on the scene (John 11:1-16). Why did Jesus know some things and not others? For instance, he told his disciples he did not know the time his heavenly Father was going to allow him to return to earth, after his departure back to the Father, as recorded in Matthew 24:36 and Mark 13:32. From my perspective, that little bit of information could not have taken that much more memory capacity to have access to, leaving the argument of a limited memory for Christ a little bit short. Could Jesus' memory on earth be limited to "X" amount of memory capacity and no more? To my understanding of the metaphysical structure of Christ, that is not likely!

Because of the complexity of these issues, we will talk more about Jesus as the God-Man in a later chapter in hopes to shed some light on how this phenomenon could take place as God designed it to be.

The Intellect of God the Holy Spirit

The Holy Spirit, as seen in our past discussions, never speaks about himself, let alone about his intellect. So what insights can we gain here to help us understand the unity of the Godhead?

Let's start with John 14:16-17, where Jesus says: "And I will ask the Father, and He will give you another Helper, that He may be with you forever; that is the Spirit of truth, whom the world cannot receive, because it does not behold Him or know Him, but you know Him because He abides with you, and will be in you." Here we learn that the Holy Spirit will not only be with you, but residing in you, as a born again believer, forever (John 3:3-6). This concept can be supported through additional study, but as we move on, we then read the following in John 16:13-15:

> But when He, the Spirit of truth, comes, He will guide you into all the truth; for He will not speak on His own initiative, but whatever He hears, He will speak; and He will disclose to you what is to come. He shall glorify Me; for He shall take of Mine, and shall disclose it to you. All things that the Father has are Mine; therefore I said, that He takes of Mine, and will disclose it to you.

Whatever the Spirit hears, he will speak. He will take of Christ's and disclose it to you. If the Holy Spirit shared all knowledge, why would anything need to be revealed to or shared with him?

This brings us back to the question: If not all members of the trinity are omniscient, are they still God? The answer to that question is, YES! Why? Because God is God because of his nature, not the attributes associated to God's personhood. **This is the most important fundamental concept within part one of this book.** If you can grasp this concept, it will allow you to understand and answer the many other questions that come to us about the triune God as we read his revelation as presented to us through the Holy Scriptures.

THE UNITY OF EMOTIONS

When we try to relate to the concept of emotions as humans, we naturally turn to our own experiences to grasp the meaning of this part of us that sometimes seems to be the weak or soft side of our humanity. Since this is a natural starting point for us, let us examine this and try to give this concept meaning with relationship to God.

As I stated in chapter three, emotions are a by-product of attitudes. It may help if we list some emotions we tend to feel or display: Agony, grieving or crying, laughing, happiness, fear and anger are all emotions we as humans have displayed. The interesting thing to notice about this list is that within Scripture, many emotions on the list are also emotions God has displayed as well. Let us examine some of them.

God the Father

The Father's demonstration of emotions can be seen in the following Scriptures. Numbers 32:14 states: "Now behold, you have risen up in your fathers' place, a brood of sinful men, to add still more to the burning anger of the Lord against Israel." Anger, as we discussed before is a product of some attitude. Because all of God's attitudes are founded in his holiness, all of God's anger and wrath is justified and right. Psalm 37:12-13 states: "The wicked plots against the righteous, And gnashes at him with his teeth. The Lord laughs at him; For He sees his day is coming." As we read this verse, we can reverse this concept and see that through God's laughter at the wicked, we can get a glimpse of his attitude toward them as well. We are told not to judge one's motives behind one's actions, but for the sake of neutral analysis for better understanding of this concept, it is my suggestion that the attitude behind this laughter is the attitude of confidence rooted in God's holiness and omnipotence. That is, God knows evil will never ultimately triumph, for he is the ultimate judge over evil; thus, his attitude of confidence based on his omnipotence and omniscience (Revelation 20:12-15; Romans 2:5-11; Isaiah 3:10-11, 32:17).

God the Son

Because we do not clearly encounter Jesus Christ as a person until his incarnation, we see his emotions as part of his humanity. It is my contention that all the emotions demonstrated by Christ, while on earth, were derived from his personhood as God. Let us review some of these as revealed to us through the Scriptures.

Mark 3:5 states: "And after looking around at them with anger, grieved at their hardness of heart, He said to the man, 'Stretch out your hand.' And he stretched it out, and his hand was restored." Here we see Jesus was not only angry but also grieved. This demonstrates to me that more than one attitude can be displayed at the same time; anger stemming from one attitude and grieving from another. Jesus was angry because of the sinful attitudes of those around him, and grieved because of the hardness of their hearts. It is my view that Jesus' attitudes stemmed from his holiness, which produced righteous indignation on one hand, while on the other, the attitude of mercy, produced grief.

Luke 19:41-42 states: "And when He approached, He saw the city and wept over it, saying, If you had known in this day, even you, the things which make for peace! But now they have been hidden from your eyes." Then again in John 11:35-37 we read, "Jesus wept. And so the Jews were saying, Behold how He loved him!" What attitudes are being displayed here? Compassion and Love! How do we know this was from the personhood of God versus a demonstration of Christ's humanity? Allow me to bring your attention to Romans 9:14-15, where we read: "What shall we say then? There is no injustice with God, is there? May it never be! For He says to Moses, I will have mercy on whom I have mercy, and I will have compassion on whom I have compassion." (For related topics, also see John 5:45-46 and Acts 3:22-26.) Jesus as God had the capacity to display these emotions and attitudes before he ever became man.

When Jesus stated in John 10:30, "I and my Father are one," just what was he referring to? The answer lies within the context of John 10. Jesus Christ and God the Father are one in power and purpose. The sheep, in reference to the text, are held by both the Father and Jesus, and none will be lost. This is a demonstration of power and purpose, which can only be unified between the two if they share the same nature, for it is God's nature or spirit that power and purpose or intentions are generated from. In the end, they are one in purpose—a product of attitude generated from their single spirit or nature.

God the Holy Spirit

Ephesians 4:30 states: "And do not grieve the Holy Spirit of God, by whom you were sealed for the day of redemption." Here we see the Holy Spirit can feel emotion of grieving. Within the context of this statement, it is our willful practicing of known sin that grieves the Holy Spirit of God. So where does this leave us within this discussion? Let us see if we can draw some conclusions to this section.

Summary of the Unity of Emotions

Jesus provides some direction for us with regard to this concept, through his prayer to the Father as found in John 17:22-23 which reads: "And the glory which Thou hast given Me I have given to them; that they may be one, just as We are one; I in them, and Thou in Me, that they may be perfected in unity, that the world may know that Thou didst send Me, and didst love them, even as Thou didst love Me."

As we review this text, we can see that God's glory, as shared with the Son and his sheep, brings unity. It is my belief that the glory shared is a product of God's nature. The Father and the Son share the same single nature or essence. God's sheep then are grafted into God's nature through the work of Christ and the Holy Spirit, allowing his sheep to partake in the unity of God's attitudes and righteousness (Romans 11:15-24; 2 Peter 1:4; Hebrews 1:1-4; 2 Corinthians 5:21), which are the controlling factors in all emotions that stem from those attitudes. Therefore, all of God's emotions, as displayed by the three persons of the trinity, are the product of all God's attitudes, which are generated by the single unifying nature of God. Therefore, God's emotions generated from his attitudes are never in conflict or contradictory within the Godhead, and are always a perfect display of God's feelings towards any person or issue.

THE UNITY OF WILL

We have spoken to the issue of "will" in chapter three. What needs to be clarified is how there can be three wills within the Godhead and still be unity? The answer to that issue is the subject matter in our next section. The short answer is that it all hinges on the concepts of God's authority and internal organizational structure that is inherent to the triune Godhead.

THE STRUCTURE OF THE SINGLE NATURE OF GOD

As we saw in chapter two, God only has one nature or spirit, and if you remember as stated earlier, it is God's nature that makes God—God. Human beings could never be God because mankind is metaphysically made different than God. By nature, God is spirit, and his nature consists of the attributes we talked about in chapter two. Each person in the trinity shares the same nature; therefore, they all share the same power, communication avenue to all forms of life, and most importantly, the same attitudes. There is no selfishness, pride, arrogance or sin of any kind found within God's nature; therefore, there are no conflicts between the tri-personhood of God. They are all holy, good, loving, unchanging and all-powerful. It is God's spirit or nature that unifies the Godhead to act and be one with each other and the universe they created. What makes this so interesting is the fact that within God there is structure and order even among the three persons. Let us look at this structure and see if we can gain any further insight into the God and creator of our universe, as he has revealed himself to us through his creation, and his written words in the canonized Scripture, as confirmed to us through the indwelling Holy Spirit of God.

God's Authoritative Structure

It is no secret in Scripture that God created everything with structure and order in mind. God does nothing without purpose! But what we may not recognize is the fact that this is true because that is how the nature of God and the personhood of the Godhead are structured. Every person in the Godhead has his place, purpose and function, with relationship to themselves and their creation. So let us examine this structure from the Scriptures, and perhaps we will gain some insight that we never thought of before.

When you think of God's authority, what do you think of? "God said it and that settles it," right? Well, that is true, but there is more to it than that. God structures his authority based on how he operates internally—that is, how each member of the trinity sees and interacts with each other. God never asks us to function in our obedience outside his personal examples. Allow me to illustrate.

God's Hierarchical Structure

The Scriptures teach that God the Father is at the top of the hierarchy within the Godhead or trinity. How do we know this? Let us start with Numbers 12:5-8:

> Then the Lord came down in a pillar of cloud and stood at the doorway of the tent, and He called Aaron and Miriam. When they had both come forward, He said, Hear now My words: If there is a prophet among you, I, the Lord, shall make Myself known to him in a vision. I shall speak with him in a dream. Not so, with My servant Moses, He is faithful in all My household; With him I speak mouth to mouth, Even openly, and not in dark sayings, And he beholds the form of the Lord. Why then were you not afraid To speak against My servant, against Moses?

As we see in these verses, it is God the Father who makes himself known, and reveals himself to the world. This line of reasoning is strengthened in Job 38:1-13 as we read:

> Then the Lord answered Job out of the whirlwind and said, "Who is this that darkens counsel By words without knowledge?" Now gird up your loins like a man, And I will ask you, and you instruct Me! "Where were you when I laid the foundation of the earth? Tell Me, if you have understanding, Who set its measurements, since you know? Or who stretched the line on it? "On what were its bases sunk? Or who laid its

cornerstone, When the morning stars sang together, And all the sons of God shouted for joy? "Or who enclosed the sea with doors, When, bursting forth, it went out from the womb; When I made a cloud its garment, And thick darkness its swaddling band, And I placed boundaries on it, And I set a bolt and doors, And I said, 'Thus far you shall come, but no farther; And here shall your proud waves stop'? "Have you ever in your life commanded the morning, And caused the dawn to know its place; That it might take hold of the ends of the earth, And the wicked be shaken out of it?

Once again, it is God the Father revealing himself and challenging Job with questions as to who designed the universe. The answer was, God the Father! Some may ask, How does this reconcile with John 1:3? The simple answer is that the triune Godhead all shares the same nature; therefore, nothing was ever made without all three being involved in the act of creation. The context of John 1:1-3 shows that Jesus and the Father are one in nature and that Jesus always existed. To the question of planning vs. acting, these are two different things. This is not to say that the other two members of the trinity had no part in the planning; only that within the planning, the Father was the head architect in charge.

Throughout the Old Testament, the main figurehead of the trinity was God the Father. The other two persons of the trinity were alluded to but not openly presented in present tense as persons. As time passed, Jesus Christ came on the scene, along with the introduction to the person of the Holy Spirit. How do these two persons fit into the triune relationship? Let us examine our knowledge base, the Scriptures.

As Jesus begins to reveal himself to us, he also reveals how he relates to God the Father. "My Father and I are one" (John 10:30); "Not my will but my father's will be done" (Luke 22:42), and the most revealing statement to this relationship is found in John 15:1: "I am the true vine; and My Father is the vinedresser." These statements reflect that the Father is in charge, and the son subjects himself to the Father. On top of this, Jesus gives us insight and examples in a lesson of submission, as we read in John 5:19-23:

> Jesus therefore answered and was saying to them, Truly, truly, I say to you, the Son can do nothing of Himself, unless it is something He sees the Father doing; for whatever the Father does, these things the Son also does in like manner. For the Father loves the Son, and shows Him all things that He Himself is doing; and greater works than these will He show Him, that you marvel. For just as the Father raises the dead and gives them life, even so the Son also gives life to whom He wishes. For not even the Father judges anyone, but He has given all judgment to the Son, in order that all may honor the Son, even as they honor the Father. He who does not honor the Son does not honor the Father who sent Him.

Wow! What revealed insight Jesus gives us to this relationship. As I stated before, God never asks us to do anything that does not take place within the Godhead. Remember the words in Scripture? "Children, obey your parents" (Ephesians 6:1), or "Wives, submit yourself to your husbands" (Ephesians 5:22, KJV), or "Husbands, love your wives" (Ephesians 5:25). These concepts come from God's personal examples, and more specifically, the Father's love for the Son and Jesus' submission to the Father. As we move on to the Holy Spirit, we see similar things. Jesus speaks in John 16:7-15, which reads:

> But I tell you the truth, it is to your advantage that I go away; for if I do not go away, the Helper shall not come to you; but if I go, I will send Him to you. And He, when He comes, will convict the world concerning sin, and righteousness, and judgment; concerning sin, because they do not believe in Me; and concerning righteousness, because I go to the Father, and you no longer behold Me; and concerning judgment, because the ruler of this world has been judged. I have many more things to say to you, but you cannot bear them now. But when He, the Spirit of truth, comes, He will guide you into all the truth; for He will not speak on His own initiative, but whatever He hears, He will speak; and He will disclose to you what is to come. He shall glorify Me; for He shall take of Mine, and shall disclose it to you. All things that the Father has are Mine;

therefore I said, that He takes of Mine, and will disclose it to you.

Again, what valuable insight Jesus gives us to see, as the Holy Spirit speaks and works according to the direction given by the Father and the Son. What was his purpose? To disclose all the Father and Son wish him to reveal. Again, we see total submission to the other two persons of the Godhead.

One side note I would like to point out: As reward for submission to the Father, the Father gives the Son full authority over all judgments over all creation (Matthew 28:18; John 17:2; John 5:22-23), and gives catastrophic punishment to those that show a certain kind of disrespect to the person and work of the Holy Spirit as spoken of in John 12:32.

God's Role Structure

It would appear that God the Father is in charge. God, throughout the Old Testament, made covenants between himself and his creation. The master plan for his creation is his. Within the New Testament, Jesus confirms this appraisal with the following statement: "My sheep hear My voice, and I know them, and they follow Me; and I give eternal life to them, and they shall never perish; and no one shall snatch them out of My hand. My Father, who has given them to Me, is greater than all; and no one is able to snatch them out of the Father's hand. I and the Father are one." (John 10:27-30) The key phrase is, "My Father, who has given them to Me, is greater than all."

In the Old Testament, we see in Genesis 1:26 God alluding to the other members of the Godhead when he spoke the words, "let us" make man in "our" image. Throughout the Old Testament, Jesus Christ and the Holy Spirit were alluded to and prophesized concerning future appearances as referenced in these passages: Luke 2:25-32; Isaiah 42:6; Galatians 3:8-9; Genesis 12:3; Jeremiah 31:31-34; Luke 24:44; Acts 3:22-26.

God's plan involving the other members of the trinity would be carried out through his covenants made to Abraham, King David and the nation of Israel. The evidence of this can be found in Genesis 12:1-3 and Genesis 17:1-8, which speak about the Abrahamic Covenant and promises that Abraham would become the father of a great nation through his son Isaac, and the land for this nation would be established forever (Psalm 105:8-12). You can find the boundaries of this land described for us in Numbers 34:1-12. Then in Second Samuel 7:10-17, we read that King David's kingdom and throne will be established forever; this is called the Davidic Covenant. Then finally we read in Jeremiah 31:31-34 that God will permanently take away the sins of his people and will dwell within them forever. This is called the New Covenant. The question is; How does God propose to accomplish all of that? The answer to that question is, through the work of Jesus Christ the Son of God, and the Holy Spirit of God, as planned and directed by God the Father.

God's covenant promises are being accomplished as we speak. How do we know this? The declaration made by Jesus Christ himself, as found in Mark 1:15 reads, "The time is fulfilled, and the kingdom of God is at hand; repent and believe in the gospel." Luke 4:43 states that preaching "the coming of the kingdom" was one purpose for Jesus coming the first time; another purpose was that he came to die (John 12:23-33). All of these purposes are a fulfillment of the Abrahamic covenant, the Davidic covenant and the New Covenant. I wish I could take the time to walk you through these arguments, but that will be left for another book.

We see the Holy Spirit's role come to light as Jesus declares for us in John 14:26-27, "But the Helper, the Holy Spirit, whom the Father will send in My name, He will teach you all things, and bring to your remembrance all that I said to you." Compare this with the words spoken through the New Covenant found in Jeremiah 31:31-34, which reads:

> But this is the covenant which I will make with the house of Israel after those days, declares the Lord, I will put My law within them, and on their heart I will write it; and I will be their God, and they shall be My people. And they shall not teach again, each man his neighbor and each man his brother, saying, "Know the Lord," for they shall all know Me, from the least of them to the greatest of them, declares the Lord, for I will forgive their iniquity, and their sin I will remember no more.

How does God put within us his laws and teach us so we know him? This all happens through the work of the Holy Spirit (Ezekiel 36:22-28, Acts 2:33-36, Romans 5:5-8, John 14:26). In retrospect, it is God, who wills and sends out the other two persons of the Godhead to fulfill all that the Father plans. I would say that this is not only perfect teamwork, but is perfect unity as well.

CONCLUDING REMARKS TO PART ONE

The danger of this type of discussion is the potential to frame God into an image that makes God less than God in our minds. This has never been my intention, nor has it been my intent to put God on a level equal to his creation. It has been my hope that what has been expressed here is an image of God that is holy, loving, all-powerful and complex in his metaphysical structure, but at the same time an image that we can understand and relate to in our own minds as God has revealed himself to us, ultimately helping us to have a better understanding of God, his nature and the nature of things.

This concludes part one of our studies concerning the image of God as the Scriptures have revealed it to us. So where do we go from here? The next few chapters will cover the nature of human beings, and how we have been altered by the change in our nature due to our choices and the sin that has befallen us. Come; join me for chapter five as we discuss the Nature of Mankind.

PART TWO:
THE IMAGE OF MANKIND

Chapter Five

THE NATURE OF MANKIND
(BODY AND SPIRIT)

Years ago when I started this study, I never took into consideration the human body as a component of human nature. This was reflected in several research papers I wrote for my Masters degree. Several months prior to writing this chapter, I was still working out the concept of the two natures of Christ that the church has historically held to since the first century, and was leaning towards Christ having only one metaphysical nature in human form. For those in the theological community, this would have been a major problem, because this view could very easily be interpreted as supporting the belief in Gnosticism. Gnostics were intellectuals that infiltrated the thinking of the early church by teaching the belief that all "matter," including the human body, was evil. Therefore, Christ only appeared as human, but was never actually human; this view was necessary, in their minds, to keep Christ holy and separated from a sinful and imperfect world.

With relationship to the subject of Gnosticism, I never held that "matter" was evil, or that Christ was not human. I simply had a different notion as to what constituted the meaning of being human. And, according to my understanding of the functions of soul and spirit, I saw no real purpose for Christ to have a human nature as defined by my definition of the term, "spirit of man." I have always held that Christ was both God and Man, but had a problem with how that worked out metaphysically. After reasoning through the model that presents two natures for Christ, I decided that this only made sense if the human body was a necessary part of mankind's human nature, as related to the death experience.

With this realization, I started to study the Scriptures concerning the human body and discovered that the body plays an important role in being human, versus just being a person of some other kind—for God represents personhood, does he not? If you remember, soulship is what makes a person a person, but what makes us a human person is tied directly to our human bodies, and I will demonstrate this through reasoning through our knowledge base, the Scriptures.

THE HUMAN BODY AS RELATED TO OUR UNIVERSE

As we have discussed in chapter four, "matter" is not evil, because it is held together by the very nature of God. The power behind the atom is God's nature as expressed in chapter two; and as we pointed out before, because there is no evil found in God (Psalm 5:4; Proverbs 8:13; 3 John 11; John 3:20), then any "matter" that God holds together by virtue of his nature cannot be evil!

We also know through our knowledge base, the Scriptures, that since the disobedience of Adam and Eve, and their transgression towards God resulting in sin (Romans 5:1-21), that God placed a curse on his creation, resulting in an irreversible decline of that same creation (Genesis 3:14-19). This is why we die and return to dust of the earth, and things decay and decline from beginning to end. From the time we are born, we begin to die physically. But within the entire process, all "matter" which exists in the universe is not evil, only under a declining change that God caused by simply changing the design rules that he created in the first place.

OUR BODIES: AN INTEGRAL PART OF HUMAN NATURE

It is stated in Genesis 2:7 that God made man out of the dust of the ground. This was man's body. If we review Genesis chapter one, there is a whole explanation on how God created every living thing after its own "kind." Man was created on the sixth day of God's seven-24-hour-day creation cycle, when God made the statement, "Let us make man in our image." No other "kind" of creature was made in God's image, only Mankind. After God created man's body and gave life to that body by breathing into it the "breath of life," we are then told that man became a living soul (KJV). Through studying the Scriptures, we find that man is made up of body, spirit and soul (First Thessalonians 5:23). But for us to understand the role of the body in our metaphysical make up, we need to examine the Scriptures for some insight on this subject. First Corinthians 15:35-39 reads:

> But someone will say, "How are the dead raised? And with what kind of body do they come?" You fool! That which you sow does not come to life unless it dies; and that which you sow, you do not sow the body which is to be, but a bare grain, perhaps of wheat or of something else. But God gives it a body just as He wished, and to each of the seeds a body of its own. All flesh is not the same flesh, but there is one flesh of men, and another flesh of beasts, and another flesh of birds, and another of fish.

As we have read, we see that the body of mankind is made differently than that of animals, birds and fish; supporting my past argument that each "kind" is different by nature. It is also evident from this passage that the body is made to change forms at God's design. (It sounds like our first law of thermodynamics all over again.) Jesus illustrates this with a parable of the mustard seed. The seed has one type of body, but after it is planted in the ground and dies, it becomes something greater and more useful (Matthew 13:31). Our bodies do play an integral part with our nature, and it is my contention that the "spirit of man," or our old sinful nature, is directly integrated to our bodies. This means that if we have no body, we have no human nature. This concept is again illustrated for us in the Scriptures as James states: "For just as the body without the spirit is dead, so also faith without works is dead" (James 2:26). Body and spirit are two separate parts, but must work together to function as a whole. Let us examine this concept to see how it all works together.

BODY AND SPIRIT AND THEIR WORKING RELATIONSHIP

As we have learned in our elementary school days, our bodies allow us access to the world through the five senses, which consist of seeing, hearing, feeling, smelling and tasting. It is the body that also gives us mobility and communications in the world through our motor skills, allowing us to speak and use our hands and feet to move about and perform tasks in the world. It is my view that when God breathed the "breath of life" into the body, at the time of creation, that this represented physical life, even though our soul came into existence at the same time (Genesis 2:7 KJV) and represents spiritual life. My conclusion to this statement comes through reasoning through Genesis 6:17, which reflects that flesh and the "breath of life" is equal to human life; John 3:3-6, which reflects a difference between the natural and the spiritual, and First Corinthians 15:35-39, which reflects the connection between the human body and its nature. At this point, we now can breathe, our heart beats, and blood flows through our bodies, but what is missing at this point is consciousness—the ability to be aware of what is around us.

So, what part of us gives us the consciousness to be aware of our surroundings? The answer is our spirit. The human body, imbedded with a human spirit, brings to us our human nature. It is our spirit, which allows us to generate and reflect attitudes and allows us consciousness of ourselves and things around us.

At this point in our discussion, we are not talking about personhood—that part of us that functions with intellect, emotion or will. Our spirit/body combination acts as our nature, just as God's spirit acts as his nature. Therefore, by this definition of mankind's nature, we can see that man is limited in his existence with relationship to God. This is why when Jesus took on a human body, he became limited to the nature of that body; even though he was still God incarnate (Hebrews 2:6-9). We will discuss this issue concerning Christ in another chapter.

Another topic or event to which the Scripture speaks with relationship to the body is the concept of the resurrection of the body. If the body has no bearing or importance to our nature, then why does God bother resurrecting it (Isaiah 26:19; Daniel 12:2; 1 Corinthians

15:13-14; John 11:24)? The Scriptures are very clear on the teaching of the resurrection of the dead. Jesus stated in John 5:28-29: "Do not marvel at this; for an hour is coming, in which all who are in the tombs shall hear His voice, and shall come forth; those who did the good deeds to a resurrection of life, those who committed the evil deeds to a resurrection of judgment." Jesus also taught us the type of change our bodies would take on in the resurrection, as recorded for us in Matthew 22:29-32: "But Jesus answered and said to them, You are mistaken, not understanding the Scriptures, or the power of God. For in the resurrection they neither marry, nor are given in marriage, but are like angels in heaven. But regarding the resurrection of the dead, have you not read that which was spoken to you by God, saying, 'I am the God of Abraham, and the God of Isaac, and the God of Jacob'? He is not the God of the dead but of the living." With all this said, it is fair to state that, like the seed that goes into the ground and dies, then comes forth something different—in like manner our bodies will also go into the ground dead, and will come forth in a new form, either to be cast into the lake of fire, or to be promoted to the new heaven and the new earth (Revelation 20:12-15; 21:1-27; Matthew 25:32-46). For a visual illustration of our nature, I leave you figure 5.1.

102 | THE NATURE OF MANKIND

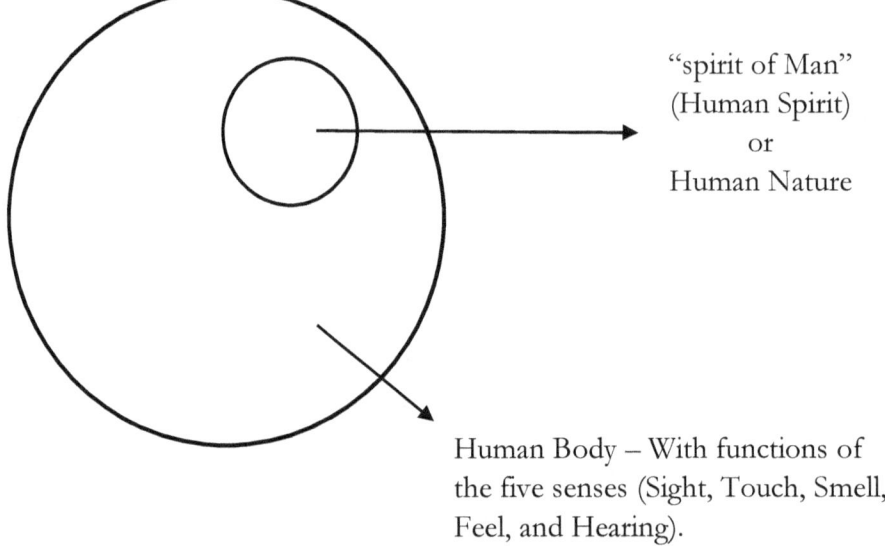

**The Metaphysical Makeup of Mankind's Nature
Figure 5.1**

As we move into the next chapter, we will build on this diagram for better understanding of the whole person of mankind. But for now, we must move into the discussion about our human nature collectively.

THE EVENTS THAT SHAPED MANKIND'S NATURE

Before the Fall or Sin

What do we know about the "spirit of man" before the fall of mankind as recorded in Genesis 3:6? Nothing! What we do know about man's spirit through the study of the Scriptures is that it is directly associated with attitude. Because we can understand God's nature and attitudes, we can conclude that man's spirit before the fall generated similar types of attitudes. Why? Because we are told in Genesis Chapter Two that man was created in God's image. We will speak to that issue in another chapter, but from what we have learned of God's image so far, we know that it is without sin or sinful attitudes.

After the Fall or Sin

At the time of Adam and Eve's choice to disobey God's instructions concerning the garden and its contents, we are told that evil had already entered the world. This evil has been recorded for us in Ezekiel 28:13-17:

> You were in Eden, the garden of God; Every precious stone was your covering: The ruby, the topaz, and the diamond; The beryl, the onyx, and the jasper; The lapis lazuli, the turquoise, and the emerald; And the gold, the workmanship of your settings and sockets, Was in you. On the day that you were created They were prepared. You were the anointed cherub who covers, And I placed you there. You were on the holy mountain of God; You walked in the midst of the stones of fire. You were blameless in your ways From the day you were created, Until unrighteousness was found in you. By the abundance of your trade You were internally filled with violence, And you sinned; Therefore I have cast you as profane From the mountain of God. And I have destroyed you, covering cherub, From the midst of the stones of fire. Your heart was lifted up because of your beauty; You corrupted your wisdom by reason of your splendor. I cast you to the ground; I put you before kings, That they may see you.

If you place this description of events into Genesis chapter three, we can see the connection between this evil one and the evil one that appeared before Eve in the garden as recorded for us in Genesis 3:1-7:

> Now the serpent was more crafty than any beast of the field which the Lord God had made. And he said to the woman, "Indeed, has God said, 'You shall not eat from any tree of the garden'?" And the woman said to the serpent, "From the fruit of the trees of the garden we may eat; but from the fruit of the tree which is in the middle of the garden, God has said, 'You shall not eat from it or touch it, lest you die.'" And the serpent said to the woman, "You surely shall not die!

"For God knows that in the day you eat from it your eyes will be opened, and you will be like God, knowing good and evil." When the woman saw that the tree was good for food, and that it was a delight to the eyes, and that the tree was desirable to make one wise, she took from its fruit and ate; and she gave also to her husband with her, and he ate. Then the eyes of both of them were opened, and they knew that they were naked; and they sewed fig leaves together and made themselves loin coverings.

Later, this connection is solidified for us through other Scripture references, such as Revelation 12:9 and 20:2.

Within the events of Genesis 3:1-7, something took place that changed the world forever. What was it that took place? And, how was it passed on to the rest of the human race? Let us see what our knowledge base, the Scriptures, has to say concerning these questions.

The Nature of the Fall

By comparing the passages we noted in Ezekiel 28:13-17 and Genesis 3:1-7, we can begin to see the nature of what happened to both the devil and Mankind.

We are told in Ezekiel 28:17 the following: "…Your heart was lifted up because of your beauty; You corrupted your wisdom by reason of your splendor…." By this statement, we can determine two very important concepts in understanding the fallen nature of the devil and subsequently mankind. The devil, through pride of his appearance, allowed his wisdom or attitude to become corrupted. If you remember, wisdom was equated to an attitude in chapter two. It was when the devil took action, according to his attitude, that his nature changed from being blameless to being unrighteous, sealing his destiny forever.

The account for what happened to mankind is identical to what happened to the devil. Genesis 3:6 reads: "When the woman saw that the tree was good for food, and that it was a delight to the eyes, and that the tree was desirable to make one wise, she took from its fruit and ate; and she gave also to her husband with her, and he ate." Satan, through the serpent's suggestion to challenge God's wisdom, set in motion Eve's attitude of pride, to be wiser than she thought she already was, for the purpose of becoming like God in equality—to have the same knowledge concerning good and evil (Genesis 3:5). Then when she and her husband took action according to each of their attitudes, they sealed their destiny and the whole worlds'. From this point on, mankind's attitudes were all enslaved to one foundational attitude, PRIDE! (Mark 7:20-22; 1 John 2:16; Proverbs 21:24; Isaiah 2:17; Job 33:16-18) And the body, being connected, became enslaved as well (Romans 8:10; 1 Corinthians 6:18; Matthew 10:28).

From this point on, Adam and Eve's nature, represented metaphysically by their spirit and body, was changed forever. Because of this change, the body also became a vehicle of change, which was to physically die and return back to the dust of the earth. This single event changed the whole world and now required God's intervention to save that which he created in his image.

We are told that the change in Adam's and Eve's nature is now passed onto all mankind through the birth process (Romans 5:13-19). We are also told that mankind's nature is equal to the nature of the devil. How do we know this? Jesus states in John 8:44: "You are of your father the devil, and you want to do the desires of your father. He was a murderer from the beginning, and does not stand in the truth, because there is no truth in him. Whenever he speaks a lie, he speaks from his own nature; for he is a liar, and the father of lies."

Some may disagree with this assessment by saying Jesus was speaking to the religious Pharisees of his day and not to the general population representing humanity as a whole. Tho it may be true that when you address an issue with a particular group of individuals, the conversation held may only apply to that group. However, Jesus is not only identifying the behaviour of a group of people, he is also identifying the nature of an attitude and its source. If anyone has lied about anything, at any time, for any reason, that person would be known as a liar. And Jesus is simply stating that lies are a product of the devil and not God by the nature of things. Therefore, because humans lie at times, they share the same nature as the devil, because he is the father of lies by nature. The end result of Jesus' statement is that we lie because we share in the same nature as the devil; for God cannot lie.

So, what is the ultimate result of this transgression or sin that was committed with relationship to our nature? Well, let us talk about that.

The Ultimate Effect of Sin on Our Nature

It is because of these facts, previously discussed, we are told both in the Old and the New Testaments the following concerning ourselves. Psalm 53:2-3 states: "God has looked down from heaven upon the sons of men, To see if there is anyone who understands, Who seeks after God. Every one of them has turned aside; together they have become corrupt; There is no one who does good, not even one." This same concept is restated in Romans 3:10-18 and reads:

As it is written,

> There is none righteous, not even one; There is none who understands, There is none who seeks for God; All have turned aside, together they have become useless; There is none who does good, There is not even one. Their throat is an open grave, With their tongues they keep deceiving, The poison of asps is under their lips; Whose mouth is full of cursing and bitterness; Their feet are swift to shed blood, Destruction and misery are in their paths, And the path of peace have they not known. There is no fear of God before their eyes.

What an indictment of the human race! Is there no hope for us? Yes! There is, but we will not get to that discussion until later. For now, we must look at how all this affects us in the here and now, within our everyday relationships, before we look at God's plan of redemption for his creation.

THE ATTRIBUTES OF THE SPIRIT OF MAN (MAN'S FALLEN NATURE)

We have learned in chapter two the concepts of God's nature. We learned that it is God's attitudes that are the controlling influence to his personhood. This same concept is true about Mankind: Our nature is also our controlling influence, as we will explore in this chapter.

As referenced in the word study results found in appendices A and B, we will look at a few verses to show that spirit, in reference to mankind, generates or reflects attitudes. Numbers 5:14 states: "And the spirit of jealousy come upon him, and he be jealous of his wife, and she be defiled: or if the spirit of jealousy come upon him, and he be jealous of his wife, and she be not defiled:" (KJV). As identified in chapter two, jealousy is an attitude. First Samuel 1:15 states: "And Hannah answered and said, No, my lord, I am a woman of a sorrowful spirit: I have drunk neither wine nor strong drink, but have poured out my soul before the Lord" (KJV). "Sorrowful" as in, "I am sad," reflects sadness, which is an attitude that can produce the emotion of crying.

To help us understand mankind's spirit, let us review part of a paragraph from chapter four, which reads:

> God's sheep then are grafted into God's nature through the work of Christ and the Holy Spirit, allowing his sheep to partake in the unity of God's attitudes and righteousness (Romans 11:15-24; 2 Peter 1:4; Hebrews 1:1-4; 2 Corinthians 5:21), which are the controlling factors in all emotions that stem from those attitudes. Therefore, all of God's emotions, as displayed by the three persons of the trinity, are the product of all God's attitudes, which are generated by the single unifying nature of God. Therefore, God's emotions generated from his attitudes are never in conflict or contradictory within the Godhead, and are always a perfect display of God's feelings towards any person or issue.

The truth we find in this paragraph concerning emotions, being a product of attitude, is also true concerning mankind. All of a person's emotions are a direct product of his or her attitudes. It is my contention, as stated earlier in this chapter, that the foundational attitude for mankind is PRIDE—just as the foundational attitude for God is LOVE based on his holiness. In the end, what I am saying is that all other attitudes displayed by man are a derivative of his PRIDE, just as all the attitudes of God are derivatives of his LOVE based on his holiness. John 3:16 tells us that God sent us his only Son to die for the penalties of our transgression or sinfulness. What was God's motive? LOVE! We saw in an earlier chapter that God displayed anger and grieved at the same time. As we noted at the time, anger stemmed from his holiness and his grief from his mercy. For God, mercy is a by-product of love.

So where does that leave mankind? Can we as human beings love, show mercy, do a kind deed? The answer to that question is a matter of perspective. Let us think through this for a moment and see if we can reason through this without a huge misunderstanding.

As we demonstrated earlier in this chapter, God sees mankind's nature as corrupt, causing mankind not to seek God (Psalm 53:2-3). As we review mankind's nature as reflected in the Scriptures, all these concepts we just talked about collectively are revealed to us in the following paragraph, as written in Ephesians 2:1-9:

> And you were dead in your trespasses and sins, 2 in which you formerly walked according to the course of this world, according to the prince of the power of the air, of the spirit that is now working in the sons of disobedience. 3 Among them we too all formerly lived in the lusts of our flesh, indulging the desires of the flesh and of the mind, and were by nature children of wrath, even as the rest. 4 But God, being rich in mercy, because of His great love with which He loved us, 5 even when we were dead in our transgressions, made us alive together with Christ (by grace you have been saved), 6 and raised us up with Him, and seated us with Him in the heavenly places, in Christ Jesus, 7 in order that in the ages to come He might show the surpassing riches of His grace in kindness toward us in Christ Jesus. 8 For by grace you have been saved through faith; and that not of yourselves, it is the gift of God; 9 not as a result of works, that no one should boast.

Within this small paragraph, we see a description of our nature as described of both flesh (body) and spirit working together in a corrupt manner; with attributes of lust and disobedience, following in like manner to the devil's attitude of Pride. It should also be noted that the whole world is walking in like manner.

It would be sad if God just walked away and left humanity in such a state. However, that's not God's attitude. Verse 4 brings us our hope as it starts with these opening two words: "But God." As you read the rest of the paragraph, we are told our hope is found in his mercy and LOVE. The God and creator of all things, provides the way to solve our dilemma concerning our nature and personhood.

Within our next chapter, we will focus back to the question of whether we can display or do any good as human beings, and hold a discussion on the issue, as we discuss the last part of our humanity, which is our personhood. So come join me for a discussion on the personhood of mankind and how that relates to the rest of our nature.

Chapter Six

THE PERSONHOOD OF MANKIND
(SOUL)

As we move into this chapter, we will be discussing several issues along with presenting several diagrams to help illustrate all that we are trying to say here. We will first cover man, as he metaphysically exists from birth. Then we will present a metaphysical representation of someone that has been grafted into the nature of God. This is the same person that Jesus terms, in John 3:3, as being born-again spiritually. Finally, we will be talking about a metaphysical representation of man after his bodily resurrection.

SOUL'S FUNCTION

The soul of man is that part of a person that displays intellect, emotion and will, which is what we discovered to be true for God. We read in Psalm 16:1-3, "Preserve me, O God: for in thee do I put my trust. O my soul, thou hast said unto the Lord, Thou art my Lord: my goodness extendeth not to thee; But to the saints that are in the earth, and to the excellent, in whom is all my delight" (KJV). This passage shows us mankind's soul, demonstrating intellect through holding a conversation with God. Jeremiah 13:17 states: "But if ye will not hear it, my soul shall weep in secret places for your pride; and mine eye shall weep sore, and run down with tears, because the Lord's flock is carried away captive"(KJV). This passage shows that our soul can demonstrate emotion through the shedding of tears. Finally, we see in Luke 1:46, Mary the mother of Jesus stating, "...My soul doth magnify the Lord...." (KJV) To magnify or worship the Lord is an act of the will.

Because man's soul functions in the same way as God's, we will not spend a lot of time looking at how the word is used in each case throughout Scripture. For further reference to how "soul" is used in Scripture, feel free to reference appendices C and D.

To provide some clarity in our minds, in reference to our discussion, I present figure 6.1.

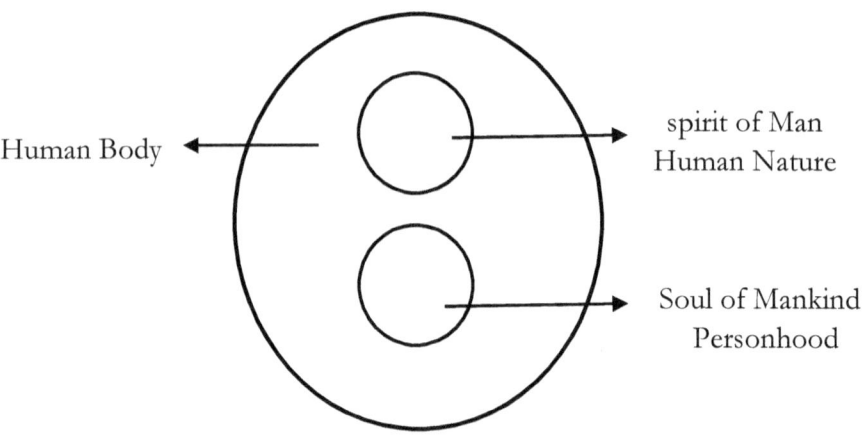

The Metaphysical Makeup of Mankind in a Natural State
Figure 6.1

DIFFERENCES BETWEEN THE SOULSHIP OF MANKIND AND GOD

Before we speak to the issue of mankind's soul, we need to talk about some differences between the soulship of mankind and the soulship of God. As we noted in chapter three, God's soulship seems to have an omnipresent mystery surrounding it, whereas mankind's soulship has no such mystery. Our soul is like all other created beings with respect to our limitations of being in a single place at any given time. This is due to having a body/spirit nature combination. Another difference is mankind's mental capacity. That is, God has the ability to maintain an infinite amount of knowledge, and mankind is limited. This can be illustrated through our knowledge base, the Scriptures. Psalm 147:4-5 states: "He counts the number of the stars; He gives names to all of them. Great is our Lord, and abundant in strength; His understanding is infinite."

Today's scientists have declared that there are trillions of stars in the heavens as we know them. Simply to hold the names for each star in a computer, could you even imagine the size computer that would be required to manage such capacity of knowledge? This is not to mention all the other knowledge within our own world to know! In contrast, man's capacity is limited by his nature—that is, man's body limits brain size, thus memory capacity. Genesis 2:20 makes a statement concerning Adam, before his sin, and states: "And the man gave names to all the cattle, and to the birds of the sky, and to every beast of the field...." We do not know if there were more or fewer species in the world at the time of creation than there are now, but no matter the case, it is certain that to give names to the amount of created species would have been a great feat even by today's standards. We are told in First Corinthians 13:9-10 the following: "For we know in part, and we prophesy in part; but when the perfect comes, the partial will be done away." At some point in mankind's history, we have lost some capacity to know fully all God wants us to know. It is my view that this loss came at the fall of mankind back in the Garden of Eden, as recorded for us in Genesis chapter three. What was it we lost? God's wisdom! And without that, we lost the ability to understand fully what God would like us to know. There will be more conversation on this as we move on to the following segments.

UNDERSTANDING THE INTELLECT OF MANKIND IN A NATURAL STATE

As discussed in the previous section, mankind's intellect is limited in comparison to God's. But part of intellect is knowledge and understanding. It is this relationship that I would like to focus on as a matter of importance to the nature of things.

It is a matter of experience that we can all obtain knowledge along life's way, but the key to that knowledge is to understand the significance or true meaning of that knowledge; for without understanding, knowledge is meaningless.

The Scriptures speak to the fact that mankind lacks understanding of knowledge in general, as well as to spiritual matters. How do we know this? First, we know this by experience, and second, we know this because the Scriptures tell us our nature works that way. Can you remember all the times in your life where you had knowledge, but you lacked understanding about how to use that knowledge, or what it really meant? I can. This is our experience as human beings. But what we may not know is that this reality is true because of our nature. Remember when we talked about the combination of wisdom plus knowledge equaling understanding? Well, let us talk further about that.

Matthew 15:10-20 states the following:

> 10 And after He called the multitude to Him, He said to them, "Hear, and understand. 11 "Not what enters into the mouth defiles the man, but what proceeds out of the mouth, this defiles the man." 12 Then the disciples came and said to Him, "Do You know that the Pharisees were offended when they heard this statement?" 13 But He answered and said, "Every plant which My heavenly Father did not plant shall be rooted up. 14 "Let them alone; they are blind guides of the blind. And if a blind man guides a blind man, both will fall into a pit." 15 And Peter answered and said to Him, "Explain the parable to us." 16 And He said, "Are you still lacking in understanding also? 17 "Do you not understand that everything that goes into the mouth passes into the stomach, and is eliminated? 18 "But the things that proceed out of the mouth come from the heart, and those defile the man. 19 "For out of the heart come evil thoughts, murders, adulteries, fornications, thefts, false witness, slanders. 20 "These are the things which defile the man; but to eat with unwashed hands does not defile the man."

It is evident through these verses, that we can have knowledge without understanding (v16). With reference to these statements of

Christ, we can see that the religious and educated rulers of his day had no spiritual understanding of their own nature (v14). The Pharisees practiced outward rituals that they believed would give them favor with God (v20). But in the end, Jesus was telling them that they were mistaken—that it was what was inside them that made the difference with God (v19-20, 1 Samuel 16:7).

If we take this one-step further, technically, what Jesus was truly telling them is that it was their motives for doing things that made them what they were. From the heart, or from their motives, evil comes. By nature, our number-one motive is PRIDE, and all other motives are derived from this one. And where do our motives come from? The answer is our spirit or nature. This is what Romans chapter 3 is talking about: "None doeth good, no, not one." This brings us to the ultimate question: Can we as sinners, in our natural state of being, do good? The really short answer is, NO! (Romans 3:9-19; Psalm 14:3) Then how does one explain all the good that takes place in the world at the hands of those still in their natural state of being? Well, as we move into this chapter, we will talk about that.

UNDERSTANDING THE EMOTIONS OF MANKIND IN A NATURAL STATE

Emotions tend to be the most misunderstood part of mankind. And why is that? Because our emotions can come to us without any understandable reasons at times! Have you ever cried, and when someone asked you, "Why the tears?" you could not give them any answer? Or, you became angry and had no understandable reason why? This is because our emotions are generated from our attitudes, and we do not always recognize what our attitudes are in relationship to what we are reacting too. The Scriptures state that our hearts are dark, which causes us not to be able to know our motives sometimes. So from God's perspective, because he is Holy and perfect, he sees our nature as corrupt and evil (John 8:44 and Psalm 53:2-3). However, the good news is, that because God is also LOVE, our soul can be saved from the evil within our nature and ultimately from God's wrath towards our nature and personhood collectively (Colossians 1:19-22).

There is a variety of emotions that humans display, and all of them stem from some attitude our nature produces. Another way of saying this is that because we have a certain attitude, some emotion we display will reflect that attitude. As an example used in earlier chapters, we know that anger is an emotion, which stems from our attitudes. With the case of mankind in his natural state, anger will always be a result of whatever attitude is generated from his nature. Since mankind's foundational attitude is PRIDE, then that will be the ultimate motive for the anger.

From man's perspective, this may not be bad. Is it not good to take PRIDE in one's work? Or even to feel good about one's accomplishments? Is not PRIDE a good motivator to achieve or drive us to do good for others? The answer would be yes if the PRIDE were rooted in God's love or nature. However, because it is rooted in Satan's nature of SELF, God sees it as evil, even when we think the result is good. The PRIDE we are referring to is the kind that tempts us to be like God—to be equal to, and thus have no need for God. We know this is true because of our previous discussions concerning the original attitude Satan and Eve had in their hearts at the beginning of creation, and as you remember, this was sealed in their nature and passed on to all mankind (Romans 5:12).

A good illustration of this concept lies with humanism. If you read the "Humanist Manifesto I" of 1933, you will find a philosophy of religious intent, that seeks to do good for the promotion and preservation of mankind, without the need for God.[1] Even though good, in the eyes of our fellow human beings, is being accomplished, the true motive for doing so is self-PRIDE, with no need for God.

Let us look at this from God's perspective. Deuteronomy 8:11-14 gives us some insight, as it reads:

> Beware lest you forget the Lord your God by not keeping His commandments and His ordinances and His statutes which I am commanding you today; lest, when you have eaten and are satisfied, and have built good houses and lived in them, and when your herds and your flocks multiply, and your silver and gold multiply, and all that you have multiplies, then your heart becomes proud, and you forget the Lord your God who

brought you out from the land of Egypt, out of the house of slavery.

PRIDE causes us to forget God even among the good times. God's intent for mankind was not for man to be on his own and live without the creator. God's intent was for us to glorify him by being and living in his image as stated in Genesis chapter two. And just what is that image? We will talk about that in chapter seven. But for now, what we need to know is God's attitude toward the proud. Proverbs 16:5 states: "Everyone who is proud in heart is an abomination to the Lord; Assuredly, he will not be unpunished." And from James 4:5-7 we read, "Or do you think that the Scripture speaks to no purpose: 'He jealously desires the Spirit which He has made to dwell in us'? But He gives a greater grace. Therefore it says, 'God is opposed to the proud, but gives grace to the humble.' Submit therefore to God. Resist the devil and he will flee from you." Within all of this, as humans, the source of our emotions is a matter of choice. But the question may come: Just what choices do we have? Let us talk about that.

Some Exceptions to the Source of Our Emotions

There are exceptions to the concept just discussed in the previous section, such as when our physical bodies are not functioning properly due to chemical imbalance. We see this in cases of women's hormones, or cases of depression, or cases of other medical reasons that our bodies are not producing the proper chemical balance for good physical or mental health. Another exception to this is, when we take drugs or alcohol that can cause us to act abnormally, either by design or as side effects. These exceptions can generate emotions outside the normal control of our nature. This is why we see warnings on medications such as, "can increase or cause thoughts of suicide." In any case, our personhood has the capacity to be influenced by outside sources—such as by other spirit beings or by chemicals. To be clear on this issue, I am neither advocating nor stating that we should not use proper medical drugs to follow a doctor's prescribed treatment. I am simply pointing out the fact that emotions can come to us through other means other than being produced through our own nature. When it comes to alcohol, the Scriptures state not to be controlled by wine, but by the power of the Holy Spirit (Ephesians 5:8; Titus 2:3).

UNDERSTANDING THE WILL OF MANKIND IN A NATURAL STATE

We have seen that the controlling factor of our intellect and our emotions is our nature. It should be no surprise then, to find the same to be true concerning our will. If you review figure 6.1, you will notice that our nature and our personhood are two different parts of our humanity.

As we think through this model, it is our nature that is corrupted, not our personhood. Therefore, there is some part of the whole person that is redeemable by God. Have you ever noticed that when the Scriptures talk about the salvation of the Lord towards mankind, in most cases, it is in reference to our soul? There is never any talk in the Scriptures to the salvation of our nature, only of our personhood. And if you remember, it is soulship that makes us a person.

Because our nature is the controlling factor of our personhood, how does that affect our will as human beings? The answer is that our will is free to choose from any attitude that is available to it within our nature. The problem is that our nature is corrupt and only has one foundational attitude from which all other attitudes derive: PRIDE. Therefore, we can never choose any motive that is acceptable to God towards righteousness or being seen as doing good before God. Isaiah 64:6 states: "But we are all as an unclean thing, and all our righteousnesses are as filthy rags; and we all do fade as a leaf; and our iniquities, like the wind, have taken us away" (KJV). The Scriptures add to this concept by stating in Romans 4:2-3: "For if Abraham was justified by works, he has something to boast about; but not before God. For what does the Scripture say? 'And Abraham believed God, and it was reckoned to him as righteousness.'"

Another behavioural factor to our human nature is revealed to us through the Apostle Paul's teaching found in Romans 6:16-18. "Do you not know that when you present yourselves to someone as slaves for obedience, you are slaves of the one whom you obey, either of sin resulting in death, or of obedience resulting in righteousness? But thanks be to God that though you were slaves of sin, you became obedient from the heart to that form of teaching to which you were committed, and having been freed from sin, you became slaves of righteousness." What Paul is telling us is that we are slaves to our sin nature that controls us. But when mankind is regenerated or born-again, we become slaves to the righteous attitudes of the new nature that the Holy Spirit brings to us through Christ. The Apostle Paul expresses this concept again in a letter to the Galatians, as he writes, "However at that time, when you did not know God, you were slaves to those which by nature are no gods. But now that you have come to know God, or rather to be known by God, how is it that you turn back again to the weak and worthless elemental things, to which you desire to be enslaved all over again?" (Galatians 4:8-9)

So if our nature prevents us from ever making the right choice, or doing the right thing before God, then how do we ever get to a place where we can please God? That is a very good question.

This takes us back to the concept of the formula: wisdom plus knowledge equals understanding. The Scriptures teach us that the only way to please God is through faith. Hebrews 11:6 states: "And without faith it is impossible to please Him, for he who comes to God must believe that He is, and that He is a rewarder of those who seek Him." So how do we have the kind of faith that God is looking for? Faith is a matter of understanding our knowledge. If we do not understand our knowledge, we tend not to believe in its truthfulness or put faith in that knowledge. Allow me to illustrate. The first step to exercising our faith toward God is that we must have some knowledge of the concept of God's existence. This is why God tells us in Romans chapter one that the creation, which he made, should be evidence enough that God does exist. God also tells us in Romans 10:17: "So then faith cometh by hearing, and hearing by the word of God" (KJV). So ultimately, the Scriptures are telling us that we must have some knowledge about God in order to exercise faith toward him. The second element required for understanding, for the purpose of exercising faith, is wisdom. If you remember from previous chapters, wisdom is an attitude that can come from either mankind or God's nature. If the wisdom is from mankind's nature, then it is a blind wisdom. If it is wisdom from God, then it is a wisdom that will lead to true understanding. How do we know this? The Scriptures state in James 3:13-17:

> Who among you is wise and understanding? Let him show by his good behavior his deeds in the gentleness of wisdom. But if you have bitter jealousy and selfish ambition in your heart, do not be arrogant and so lie against the truth. This wisdom is not that which comes down from above, but is earthly, natural, demonic. For where jealousy and selfish ambition exist, there is disorder and every evil thing. But the wisdom from above is first pure, then peaceable, gentle, reasonable, full of mercy and good fruits, unwavering, without hypocrisy.

The type of wisdom or attitudes expressed here comes from two different natures. Because mankind's wisdom comes from his own nature, he will never come to a spiritual understanding of biblical truth, even if knowledge is present. For without God's wisdom, man's knowledge is incomplete to exercise faith. There are theological systems that say God must give us our faith toward salvation. According to my understanding of what the Scriptures are revealing to us, faith is ours to exercise, but we lack the understanding to exercise it. This can be verified throughout the Gospels, as Jesus states many times, let it be according to your faith or your belief in the matter at hand as the following Scriptures reflect: (Matthew 6:30; 9:2; 9:22; 9:29; 15:28; 17:20; Mark 5:34; 10:52; Luke 5:20; 7:50; 17:19; 18:42). The Apostle Paul made similar statements as found in Romans 1:8, Second Corinthians 1:24 and Colossians 1:4.

Therefore, we have free will to exercise our faith toward any concept we choose within the scope of our human nature; the problem is that God is not included in that scope. Mankind's nature can never produce the wisdom required to understand God's standards of holiness, thus can never come to an understanding of the salvation process for reconciliation. So what is the answer? Somehow, we need a new nature that can give us the wisdom to understand God's ways. With that said, come join me for the second half of our discussion.

THE START TO MANKIND'S RECONCILIATION OF BEING

The Scriptures are clear that Salvation of Mankind is of the Lord (Psalm 3:8; Genesis 49:18; Acts 4:12). Another way to say this is that it is God who must give us the wisdom to understand his salvation message, so we can choose by faith to act on that message (Job 32:8). Therefore, it is God who must step into our lives through LOVE and mercy and give us the gift of his wisdom, that we may exercise our faith in the Gospel of Jesus Christ. This is what the Scriptures call GRACE. Thus, in the end, salvation comes to us by the grace of God alone (Ephesians 2:8).

So, by God providing us wisdom through the presents of the Holy Spirit, applied to the knowledge of the Gospel, we then come to a true understanding of God's message, allowing us to exercise a willful act of repentance towards God and faith in the work of Jesus Christ (Acts 20:18-21).

So if we exercise our faith in Christ, what happens to our nature that makes us new creatures in Christ (2 Corinthians 5:17)? Does our nature change and we become perfect? To help us understand what it means to have a new nature in Christ, let us examine figure 6.2 below.

UNDERSTANDING MANKIND'S CHANGED STATE OF BEING

Upon man's new understanding of the Gospel (2 Peter 1:1-4), through God's free gift of wisdom, a true choice can now be made toward repentance and faith in Jesus Christ the righteous. If through God's wisdom, mankind makes the choice toward repentance and faith in Jesus Christ, God's only son, then an adoption or new spiritual birth takes place (Ephesians 4:24; 2 Corinthians 5:17; Romans 8:15-16), and mankind receives a new spiritual nature (Acts 14:15; 2 Peter 1:4). This new nature becomes permanent (John 14:16-17)—and we will talk about that—and is one that gives mankind additional choices that can please God. Thus, by faith, we now possess two natures, and a need to have a better understanding of mankind's dual-nature role and eternal future.

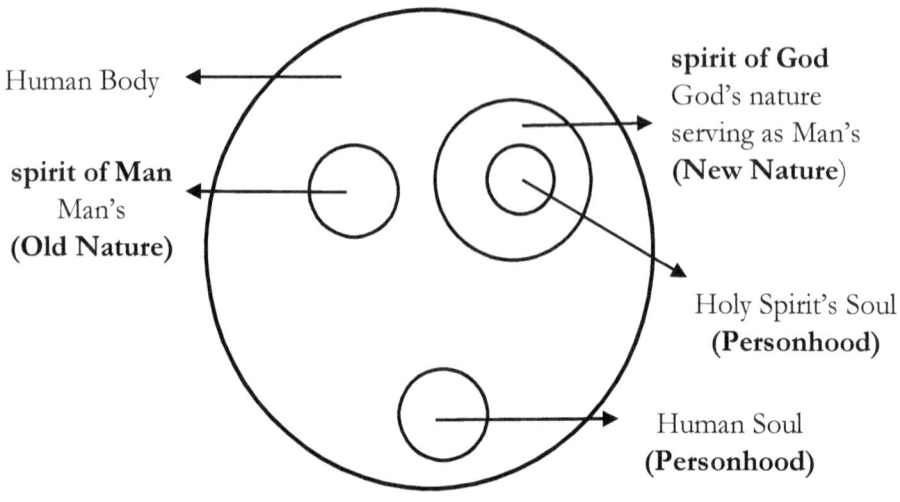

The Metaphysical Makeup of Mankind in a New State
Figure 6.2

    There is an argument within the study of theology that would state that God gives us our faith, and the freedom of choice or will has nothing to do with the salvation process. My response to that viewpoint is to support my position through the review of the life of King Solomon. The Scriptures state that Solomon was the wisest man that ever has or will ever live (1 Kings 3:7-12). The wisdom given was a gift of God's—and even after God's lifelong gift, Solomon still had to make choices in the use of that gift to do right or wrong. As we read about the life of Solomon, we would discover that towards the end of his life, he chose to do evil in the sight of the Lord (First Kings 11:6).

    The moral of the story is, even when we are no longer blind to God's truth because of God's wisdom in us, the human will must still be exercised to make right or wrong choices. The argument that we only choose sin because we are spiritually blind holds no water with the example of King Solomon, who understanding truths about God, still chose to be disobedient to God. Why? PRIDE! And the same wisdom God gave Solomon is the same wisdom he gives us to reveal his truth concerning salvation. Therefore, just because God gives people his gift of wisdom for understanding spiritual truth, does not mean people will exercise their will and choose God. This line of thought is supported through Jesus' parable of the sower found in Matthew 13:10-23. With a closer examination of this parable you will find that understanding was not enough for God's seed to take hold; it required action to produce fruit that sealed the deal. This was the act of the will after understanding took place. Something to think about!

This is the ultimate meaning to the phrase "the sovereignty of God and the responsibility of Man." Without God's wisdom, we cannot choose God, and after God's gift of wisdom, we must still make a choice.

I would like to stress the point that the gift of wisdom is not the factor that saves us from our sins, but is the factor that gives us the ability to choose faith in Christ alone—this is the Gospel message—to repent of our sinfulness and place our faith in Christ alone. Without God stepping in and opening our spiritual eyes to see the truth of the Gospel message, through his gift of wisdom, we could never willfully make a choice to choose salvation; this is why this whole process is called GRACE. It is by the grace of God that wisdom is ever offered to humanity.

The view just expressed holds a much broader support of the Scriptures as a whole, than the view of humanity having no free will to exercise at all. Remember, for biblical truth to be true it must agree with all other biblical truth. Something to think about!

UNDERSTANDING MANKIND'S DUAL NATURE

We have already mentioned, in chapter five, mankind's old nature as referenced in the Scriptures as the "spirit of man." The difference between figures 6.1 and 6.2 is the addition of a new nature. This new nature is provided to us through the work of the Holy Spirit of God (2 Timothy 1:14). Our new nature is actually God's spirit, as the person of the Holy Spirit brings it to us. To aid us in a better understanding of this phenomenon let us walk through the Scriptures to see just how all this works.

If we review chapter two of this book, we would see that God's nature is that part of God that has power to create and work miracles in the universe. We would also see that it is that part of God that provides communication to all other spirit beings, and generates attitudes. Through the Holy Spirit coming to indwell believers in Christ, some of these same attributes become ours for use as reflected in the following Scriptures: Romans 15:13; Hebrews 6:4; First Corinthians 12; Acts 1:8.

Understanding New Choices

As you examine figure 6.2, you will see two natures represented. If you think through the functions of these natures, you will soon understand that our personhood, with the functions of intellect, emotion and will, now has choices between which nature or attitudes to display and follow. This also brings us the element of conflict within us—a battle between our natures that wages in our mind and soul (Romans 7:14-25, 12:1-2; 2 Corinthians 10:3-6; James 4:1-8).

With this model before us, let us plug in some Scripture references to see if they begin to make better sense to us for understanding God and ourselves as believers in Christ (Christians).

James 4:1-8 says:

> What is the source of quarrels and conflicts among you? Is not the source your pleasures that wage war in your members? 2 You lust and do not have; so you commit murder. And you are envious and cannot obtain; so you fight and quarrel. You do not have because you do not ask. 3 You ask and do not receive, because you ask with wrong motives, so that you may spend it on your pleasures. 4 You adulteresses, do you not know that friendship with the world is hostility toward God? Therefore whoever wishes to be a friend of the world makes himself an enemy of God. 5 Or do you think that the Scripture speaks to no purpose: "He jealously desires the Spirit which He has made to dwell in us"? 6 But He gives a greater grace. Therefore it says, "God is opposed to the proud, but gives grace to the humble." 7 Submit therefore to God. Resist the devil and he will flee from you. 8 Draw near to God and

He will draw near to you. Cleanse your hands, you sinners; and purify your hearts, you double-minded.

By reviewing this passage of Scripture, we see that the problem in this conflict is motives (v3). We also see that God desires us to make the right choices (v5). And finally, we see that submitting to God and making choices that draw us closer to him will aid us in the battle of being double-minded (v8), or always flip-flopping back and forth between the attitudes provided by the two natures within us. In the end, our choices are motivated by PRIDE (v3) or HOLINESS and Love (v8).

John 14:26 states: "But the Helper, the Holy Spirit, whom the Father will send in My name, He will teach you all things, and bring to your remembrance all that I said to you." This Scripture is very interesting to me because it tells me that my new nature through the Holy Spirit has the ability to help me recall memory or knowledge. This also tells me that if God can do this to influence my personhood, so can Satan do the same through my old nature. This takes us back to our discussion of God sending an evil spirit upon King Saul. Because we are spiritual beings, we have the capacity to be influenced by the spirit world through our natures.

This line of thinking then leads us into the natural questions of demon influence. The Old Testament Scripture references demon influence in Leviticus 17:7, Deuteronomy 32:17 and Psalm 106:37. Within the New Testament we see Jesus casting out demons and giving his disciples the authority to do the same (Matthew 4:24; 8:16; 10:1; Mark 3:22; Luke 4:41). The concepts of a devil and demons are taught plainly in Scriptures and make sense with relationship to our human nature, and how our spirits work with relationship to our personhood.

The Apostle Paul made this comment concerning this issue in First Corinthians 10:20-22: "No, but I say that the things which the Gentiles sacrifice, they sacrifice to demons, and not to God; and I do not want you to become sharers in demons. You cannot drink the cup of the Lord and the cup of demons; you cannot partake of the table of the Lord and the table of demons. Or do we provoke the Lord to jealousy? We are not stronger than He, are we?" What this passage tells us is that, we have the capability to communicate to both spirit worlds in our

"New State." It is also clear from this passage that it is God's desire that we have no communications with the demon world. That is, we should not be praying, worshiping, or sacrificing to the demon world, which is ultimately the kingdom world of Satan (Matthew 12:26). This concept would also forbid the practices of witchcraft, spiritists or mediums as declared to us in Deuteronomy 18:9-13.

Another question may arise from this discussion is, Can we in a "New State" be overtaken and possessed by the demon world? To answer that question I will turn to Jesus' teaching in Luke 11:21-23 which states: "When a strong man, fully armed, guards his own homestead, his possessions are undisturbed; but when someone stronger than he attacks him and overpowers him, he takes away from him all his armor on which he had relied, and distributes his plunder. He who is not with Me is against Me; and he who does not gather with Me, scatters."

This teaching which appears in all the synoptic gospels (Matthew 12:29, Mark 3:27), tells us that the strongest man in the room wins in any hand-to-hand conflict. To take over the house, the strongman must be beaten. This story was given to us to help us see that God is stronger than Satan, and that we must choose sides. Therefore, if the Holy Spirit resides in us, then there is no place in our spiritual house for any other spirit being to reside in that could be any stronger. Based on this teaching, it is my view that the person that has been sealed by the Holy Spirit is permanently the temple of his, and that no other spirit can reside there. This does not mean we cannot be influenced by Satan or demons; it just means we cannot be controlled through physical possession. The most fitting Scripture that fits our discussion on this issue is found in First John 4:4, and reads: "Ye are of God, little children, and have overcome them: because greater is he that is in you, than he that is in the world" (KJV).

Understanding the Permanency of Our New Nature

The starting point to understanding the question, "How long will we have the Holy Spirit residing in us?" lies with understanding the foundational concept as to why this phenomenon is happing in the first place.

Jeremiah 31:31-34 states:

> Behold, days are coming, declares the Lord, when I will make a new covenant with the house of Israel and with the house of Judah, not like the covenant which I made with their fathers in the day I took them by the hand to bring them out of the land of Egypt, My covenant which they broke, although I was a husband to them, declares the Lord. But this is the covenant which I will make with the house of Israel after those days, declares the Lord, I will put My law within them, and on their heart I will write it; and I will be their God, and they shall be My people. And they shall not teach again, each man his neighbor and each man his brother, saying, "Know the Lord," for they shall all know Me, from the least of them to the greatest of them, declares the Lord, for I will forgive their iniquity, and their sin I will remember no more.

These are the words of the New Covenant in which the New Testament is based. God made a permanent, everlasting covenant with the nation of Israel, and through a grafting in process, as spoken of in Romans 11:25-33, the gentiles are grafted in as well. This covenant is unconditional—that is, there are no provisions for us to fulfill; it all rests on God's promise and commitment to save his creation. It is this covenant, which provides the purpose for the indwelling of the Holy Spirit to take place. For without the Holy Spirit, we can never know God in a personal way. If you review figure 6.2, you will be able to see, in a metaphysical way, how we can know God, and take part in his Holiness and Love. Remember, it is the nature of God that brings us communications and all the attitudes that God provides; we can see this through the fruit of the Spirit as represented in Galatians 5:22.

From this concept, Jesus tells us that after he leaves this world through his ascension (Acts 1:6-11), he will send us another helper (the Holy Spirit) and he will be with us forever (John 14:6). Why forever? Because God's words, as spoken through the New Covenant, are forever! God gave the Holy Spirit as a pledge of our inheritance. Ephesians 1:13-14 states that the Holy Spirit of promise seals us. If the Holy Spirit could leave us, then God's pledge or promise would be meaningless, making God a liar. We are told in Ephesians 4:30 that we are sealed for the day of redemption. Our redemption is complete at the time of our resurrection—or, if Christ returns during our lifetime, our ascension, if you believe in the doctrine of the rapture.

There are those that teach that one can lose this sealing by not staying the course or on the right path with God. The answer to that issue is threefold. First, the Scriptures teach that it is God that saves and keeps us to the day of redemption, lest we make Jesus' death, burial, and resurrection null and void (Romans 4:14). Second, Jesus makes this declaration in John 10:27-30: "My sheep hear My voice, and I know them, and they follow Me; and I give eternal life to them, and they shall never perish; and no one shall snatch them out of My hand. My Father, who has given them to Me, is greater than all; and no one is able to snatch them out of the Father's hand. I and the Father are one." If we insist on the claim that one can lose their salvation, then we are calling Jesus the Son of God a liar! (The key to this argument is, let us be sure one has been saved to start with.) And third, there is a doctrine that many of us miss—but exists all the same—and that is that within God's nature, which resides in all those that have been adopted or born-again, is the concept that God cannot deny himself (2 Timothy 2:13). What does that mean? It means that if God is living inside you through your new nature, then he will not allow you to deny himself or his precepts. To act, and walk away from God in denial, is an act of denying God. This would be apostasy. This cannot happen to those that are truly born-again in the first place. The Scriptures teach that our new nature will give us the desire to please God, not walk away from his presence. Something to think about! (Galatians 5:16-24; Romans 6:14-23)

The result of this argument does not mean God's people do not sometimes drift away from God's standards on a temporary basis. It simply means God's people will always be mindful of God's standards and be convicted of them until they repent and place themselves back in line to God's standards. A person that denounces God is a person that most likely will not sense any conviction to return. Why? Because this is the work of the Holy Spirit (John 14:16-17, 26; 16:8-11)! If the Holy Spirit was not present to keep you from denial in the first place, then it is likely that the Holy Spirit will not be present to convict you either. If this does not seem reasonable to you, then feel free to search the Scriptures for the truth, for the truth is our ultimate goal.

UNDERSTANDING OUR NATURE AFTER THE RESURRECTION

We now enter an area that I have spent many hours thinking through, and can say that we are about to enter an area that is a mystery to us and not yet fully understood. Nevertheless, I feel this is an area we can reason through and come close to what may be reality, with relationship to the topic of our nature after the resurrection.

The Scriptures use the term "regeneration" in Matthew 19:28 and Titus 3:5. If you study this term within theology, you will find that it is used synonymously with the spiritual new birth. It also can refer to a new state of being or a renewal of one's spiritual state. Matthew 19 is referencing a new spiritual state of existence, and in Titus, it is used in reference to a new spiritual birth. As we review figure 6.3, unregenerated mankind consists of all human beings that have never experienced a new spiritual birth, as described by Jesus Christ in John chapter three. Regenerated mankind includes all human beings that have willingly experienced all that Jesus Christ is expressing in John chapter three concerning the new birth.

We are not going to spend a lot of time here, but I do want to touch on some concepts concerning what we become metaphysically after the resurrection of the dead, which the Scriptures make reference to many times. Let us walk through the concept of unregenerated mankind and see what kind of light the Scriptures can shed on this subject.

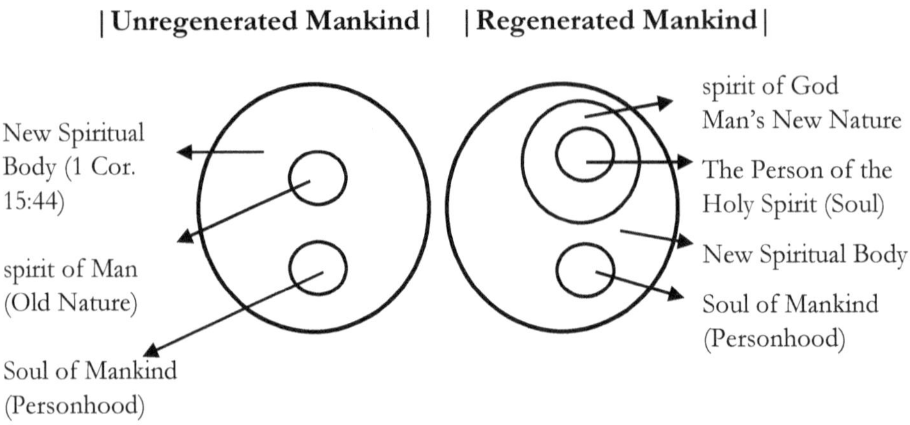

130 | *THE PERSONHOOD OF MANKIND*

|Unregenerated Mankind| |Regenerated Mankind|

New Spiritual Body (1 Cor. 15:44)

spirit of Man (Old Nature)

Soul of Mankind (Personhood)

spirit of God Man's New Nature

The Person of the Holy Spirit (Soul)

New Spiritual Body

Soul of Mankind (Personhood)

The Metaphysical Makeup of Mankind in a Resurrected State
Figure 6.3

UNREGENERATED MANKIND

Unregenerated Body

We know through funeral cremations that our body can be harmed and even incinerated to ashes if placed in a hot enough oven. We also know from Revelation 20:11-15 that judgment will come to the world of unregenerated mankind and end up in a final state of death in the "lake of fire." It is my view that the human bodies resurrected in Revelation 20 are not the same as what they were during life on earth the first time around. Why? Because the heat would be so intense that the original body would never survive the punishment. We have already seen through the Scriptures that the body will change in the resurrection by God's design (1 Corinthians 15:35-44). But within the Christian community, the talk is always of the Glorified body of Christ, and those that become regenerated in him. It is my view that the lost or the unregenerated will also receive different types of bodies, the kind that will not be able to be burned up in fire, but will still afford all the functions of the five senses that the body has always provided. This is stated in First Corinthians 15:35-44. We can also see this in the story Jesus tells us concerning the rich man in hell, who is asking that someone tell his brothers, back in the living world, about his torment, with the purpose of warning. If we look at the story, it stated that the man felt pain, could see, could hear, could speak, and was thirsty (Luke 16:22-26).

Some could argue that this is just a story Jesus told to prove a point or teach some spiritual lesson to the Pharisees. I believe within this story is found a true reality of facts, even if the event never took place and was used as a teaching tool, as parables were. It is my view that this story, by using real names of real people represents not a parable, but a real event shared with us to teach us earthly and spiritual principles that can be used to evaluate other information in Scripture and aid us in our reasoning about other true concepts within Scripture. This can be supported simply by reading a good Bible commentary or the hermeneutical books referenced in chapter one.

Unregenerated Soul

If we continue to review the story that Jesus told in Luke 16, we would find that all the functions of the soul are still intact. The rich man was in anguish, demonstrating emotions; holding a conversation with Abraham, demonstrating intellect; and asking for water and for someone to go to his family, demonstrating an act of the will.

We also can see that the rich man still had his memory. He had a remembrance of his family and past actions that took place in his earthly life, as Abraham reminded him of his good life of luxury in comparison to that of Lazarus.

Unregenerated Spirit

It is the "spirit" part of man's nature that has always eluded me in my understanding in relation to Christ, and life after death. For me, this element of the equation, metaphysically, will always be a mystery to me, and I may never come to a 100% certainty concerning its purpose of function in either scenario. All the same, we must talk about this spirit's destiny in the end.

If you remember, the "spirit of man" serves as mankind's old sinful nature. In reference to Jesus' story in Luke 16, we see that the rich man was displaying an attitude, one of concern for his family, but why he was concerned is the issue. It is my view that no matter what his motive may have been in his mind, it stemmed from the ultimate motive of his nature, PRIDE. How can we say this? Because we have already determined that PRIDE is the ultimate motivator of the unregenerated human being. And if he had become regenerated, he would not have been in the place he found himself to be in.

REGENERATED MANKIND

Regenerated Body

First Corinthians 15:35-44 speaks about the concepts of an earthly body and a heavenly body, but even among these resurrected bodies, there is indication that there could be a difference. If we read this Scripture and review its content, we would see that by the concepts being presented here, we could expect that the bodies of the unregenerated and regenerated could be different in some way not yet understood. It also could mean that Christ's body could be something different than what the regenerated would receive. It is truly a mystery that we will never know on this side of life. But in the end, regenerated mankind will receive a body that has its own glory as expressed in chapter 15, and function with the five senses of the body, as it does now. We know this because the Scriptures tell us of events in the future that demonstrate such functions (Revelation chapters 21 and 22).

Regenerated Soul

If we examine Revelation chapter 21 and 22, we can see a new state of existence, and the act of worship means that there will be the functions of intellect, emotion and will—for all three are required in the act of worship. In relation to memory, there are several things to consider. One, God states in the New Covenant that he will not remember our sins. If God can block his memory of our sins, do you believe we will remember them in a regenerated life? Not likely. To do so would mean we could feel sadness resulting in weeping. Revelation 21:4 states that all this will be done away with; therefore, remembrance of past transgression is not likely—not to mention, if God has forgotten, will he allow you to remind him? Sounds rather silly, does it not? This is in great contrast to those in an unregenerated state, whom the Scriptures say will be in a state of wailing and gnashing of teeth (Matthew 13:43-50; Luke 13:22-28).

Regenerated Spirit

It is this portion of our study that brings me the most curiosity to what is, or what may be. It is my view that, after the resurrection of the regenerated person, the "spirit of man" is no longer required, neither in function nor in purpose. Let us talk about this.

As we know, spirit is that from which attitude is generated. We read in Revelation 21:4 that God will remove all death, sorrow, pain and tears from our personhood. What this means is that we are different, to include our nature. We know that our bodies have changed, which is part of our nature—but what happens to the other part of our nature, our spirit? There are two views one can take. One, our spirit is changed back to what Adam once had before the fall. Or second, our spirit no longer exists or resides within us. Through reviewing figure 6.3, my position on this issue has been declared. Allow me to give some explanation to my thoughts on this issue.

We are told in Revelation 21 that we will have a different nature. We know this by reasoning through the function of that nature. If we cannot die, be sad, or cry due to sadness, then our nature has changed, in both a physical and spiritual way. Therefore, for this to take place, not only must our bodies change, but our attitudes as well. We can no longer have an attitude of PRIDE. For this to take place in us, either our spirit must change to its original state before the fall, or that spirit no longer exists or resides in us. If we think through the function of spirit, our new nature provides all the function we need to continue on as human beings. Without our old nature, we will no longer have all the evil motives to choose from that we once had, and therefore our choice to sin will no longer be possible.

It is at this time that I would like to provide the answer to the ultimate question we spoke of in chapter two. This study was started on the primary question as to what is life. The answer comes when we examine the purpose of the "spirit of man" which came from God. One purpose is to provide life or consciousness to our personhood. How do we know this? Ecclesiastes 12:7 states: "Then shall the dust return to the earth as it was: and the spirit shall return unto God who gave it" (KJV). Spirit is a product of God. So, one part of our nature goes back to dust, and the other goes back to God, the owner of it.

When Jesus states in John 14:6 that he is the life, or in John 11:25 that he is the resurrection and the life, Jesus is not saying that he is the provider of life, or that he is simply the way to eternal life. What Jesus is ultimately saying is that he is everlasting life itself for the regenerated person. His very metaphysical spirit essence provides us eternal life. Therefore, by receiving the spirit of God, we are receiving life itself that has no end in the presence of God. This may help us understand Jesus statement to his disciples in John 6:54-56, which reads: "He who eats My flesh and drinks My blood has eternal life, and I will raise him up on the last day. For My flesh is true food, and My blood is true drink. He who eats My flesh and drinks My blood abides in Me, and I in him." The Scriptures go on to state that this statement was so difficult for those listening, that some who were following his ministry stopped following. Jesus' explanation of his statement was expressed in verse 63 when he said: "It is the Spirit who gives life; the flesh profits nothing; the words that I have spoken to you are spirit and are life." It is my view that spirit and life are one in the same and therefore, Jesus was trying to say within his flesh and blood statement, that if we do not partake in literally receiving his spirit nature, which the Holy Spirit brings to us, we will have no eternal life with him, physically or spiritually.

If this is the case, then our new nature can provide all the same functions that our old nature can within in our new resurrected state. It is because of these facts I have always had a dilemma with the two natures of Christ, and will discuss this topic in another chapter.

And finally, we have the statement that the Holy Spirit will be in us forever (John 14:6)—which is the decisive factor for me on this topic, because it raises the question: Why is the indwelling of the Holy Spirit necessary after the resurrection? My only conclusion is that our new nature will permanently replace our old nature. However, if our old nature was renewed and restored to what it once was before the fall, what function would it provide? It would duplicate all the same functions our new nature provides through the permanent indwelling of the Holy Spirit. This follows the same line of discussion we had concerning Jesus and his human spirit nature. Does Jesus need a human spirit after his resurrection? So goes my dilemma—Why the duplication when there is no need for it? This discussion will be continued in our next chapter as we talk about being made in the image of God.

Well, we finally made it to a place where we can have a discussion on what it means to be made in the image of God. Within our next chapter, we will talk about two concepts that run parallel to each other, and hopefully I have conveyed enough information so that chapter seven will make sense to you in our journey to understanding the natures of God and Mankind.

As we discover the reality of what it really means to be made in the image of God, I trust that this knowledge will be of some benefit to your life in a changing way. So come, join me for Chapter 7, and let us press on in our journey to understanding the nature of things.

CHAPTER SIX ENDNOTES

[1] http://americanhumanist.org/Humanism/Humanist_Manifesto_I (Added for additional reference to the reader.)

Blank Page

PART THREE:
MANKIND MADE IN THE IMAGE OF GOD

Chapter Seven

THE LIKENESS AND IMAGE OF MANKIND

Part one of this book allowed us some insight into the nature of God by examining God's nature through an image of his metaphysical existence. Part two of this book allowed us some insight to the nature of Mankind and a metaphysical reflection of its image. As we navigate through this chapter, we will review what we have learned and begin to compare these images for similarities and differences. As this chapter progresses, we will begin to see an image emerging that will illustrate what God meant by his statement as found in context of Genesis 1:26-27, which reads as follows:

> Then God said, "Let Us make man in Our image, according to Our likeness; and let them rule over the fish of the sea and over the birds of the sky and over the cattle and over all the earth, and over every creeping thing that creeps on the earth." And God created man in His own image, in the image of God He created him; male and female He created them.

GOD'S IMAGE REVIEWED

As we examine the verses above, we see God begins his statement as follows: "Let Us make man in Our image, according to Our likeness." The first question that comes to my mind is, just what is the image of

God? As important as that question is, an equally important question is, what does it mean to be in God's likeness? It is this second question that deals with a metaphysical issue, and one we need to deal with first. God went on in Genesis 1:27 to qualify his statements by applying "image" to both male and female human beings. This is a very important qualifier because it demonstrates that God is not speaking of mankind's anatomical body structure. God is speaking to our metaphysical and moral attributes. To illustrate this in a visual way, let us examine figure 7.1.

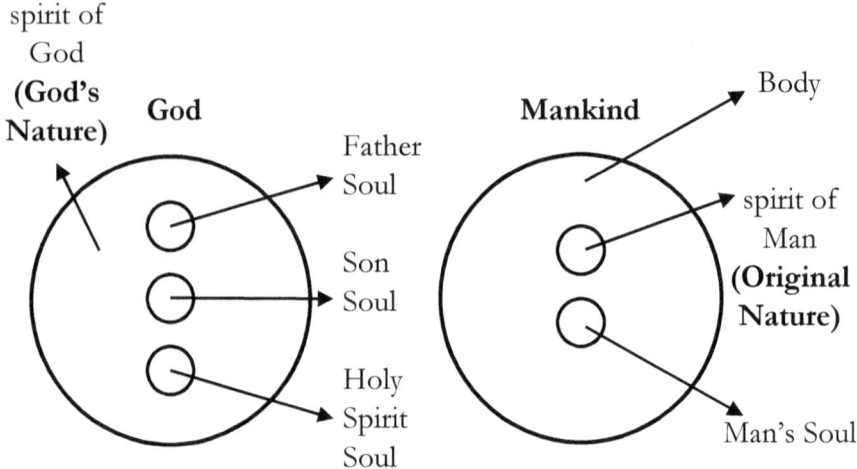

The Metaphysical Similarities of God and Mankind before Sin
Figure 7.1

As the diagram illustrates, God is spirit (John 4:24), and unlimited in his presence. God's spirit has no boundaries, as discussed in chapter two. On the other hand, mankind is material or natural (1 Corinthians 15:46); that is, mankind has a physical presence that is limited by his body. With regard to these differences, there is no image reflection. As we examine the image of mankind's soul and spirit to God's, we begin to see a likeness, which we will speak to later in this chapter.

To summarize God's image as presented in part one, we have redrawn God's metaphysical makeup in figure 7.1 for your review, and understand the following to be true. We know that God is spirit, and furthermore is omnipresent. We also know that this spirit carries attributes of power and communications, as well as being that part of God that functions as the controlling factor of his personhood, through the reflections and the generation of attitudes. We know that God is holy and loving, among other things, which is the result of the makeup and function of God's spirit or nature.

As to God's soul or personhood, we know that God is three persons, and all three persons possess and display intellect, emotions and will. We also know that God's personhood also carries with it additional ontological attributes.

It is these parts of God's image we want to evaluate with relationship to mankind's image.

MANKIND'S IMAGE REVIEWED BEFORE SIN

Mankind's image is made up of his body, soul and spirit, as expressed in part two of this book. We know that man's soul demonstrates intellect, emotion and will. We also know that man's spirit is where his attitudes are generated from, and where his conciseness operates.

It is through this knowledge that we can begin to evaluate similarities between God and Mankind, to aid in our understanding to what God is talking about in his statements made in Genesis 1:26-27.

SIMILARITIES OF BOTH IMAGES BEFORE SIN

As we begin to compare similar attributes of both God's and Man's soul and spirit, we can see that both are in some likeness with relationship to functionality and purpose. Let us go over these similarities and see what we can determine through reasoning through our knowledge base thus far.

God and Mankind's souls both work in the same manner; they both function with intellect, emotion and will. The soul is also that part of each entity that determines personhood. Some differences are that God has unlimited power and capacity for memory and understanding, whereas mankind is limited in his memory and understanding. It is my contention that this is true because of the difference between their natures. That is, God is spirit, making him metaphysically unlimited in his capacity of presence, power, communications and wisdom. Through God's design of the human body, man is limited in his capacity in areas of presence, communications, memory, wisdom and power. So how are we in God's likeness? We are in God's likeness by design of our spirit and soul. Allow me to expand this thought with some illustrations.

God did not create our spirit or soul like he did our bodies. Our spirit and soul are products of God's essence. Allow me to clarify this statement by restating it another way: God is spirit, and God created our spirit/soul parts from the same design as his. Our spirit is not made from his, but was made in structural form to be and function like his. How do we know this? The Scriptures state that God made our bodies out of the dust of the ground. This is physical. But when it came to producing a living soul or being, the Scriptures state that God breathed into the body this unknown quantity called life (Genesis 2:7). This means that life is a direct product of God himself. That is, our spirit and soul are made up of the same properties as God's. Allow me to illustrate this. If God's spirit were made of water, then in like manner our spirit would be made of water. If God's soul were made of gold, then our soul would be made of gold. By design, God made mankind in a metaphysical likeness of himself. You might say that we are clones of God's metaphysical design. Therefore, our soul and spirit look and function like God's, but these parts do not add up to be God, as God and Mankind are of two different natures. Our spiritual makeup is made to look and function just like God the creator's. This is why our soul never dies and our spirit returns back to God who gave it (Ecclesiastes 12:7; Revelation 20). Someone may ask: Why is there no death to these parts? And the answer would be, because God is eternal, and anything God creates in a spirit life form becomes eternal. We know this to be true because both humans and fallen angels have an eternal judgment to face (Revelation 20). If this is true, then how should we understand the concept of death?

THE CONCEPT OF DEATH IN THE SCRIPTURES

Within the Scriptures listed here, we can find the concept of the soul dying or being killed (Psalm 33:19; Psalm 63:9; James 5:20). So how should we view this? When the Scriptures speak on the death of a soul, it is speaking on two levels. First, it is speaking to physical death; and second, it is speaking to spiritual death—that is, spiritual death refers to the soul suffers in an eternal conscious punishment of burning pain. How do we know this? Let us start by looking at Matthew 10:38, which states: "And fear not them which kill the body, but are not able to kill the soul: but rather fear him which is able to destroy both soul and body in hell" (KJV). Within this verse, Jesus informs us that man can kill the body but cannot harm the soul, even after the body is dead—meaning that the soul lives on even after the body has died. Nevertheless, God has the authority and power to place the soul in hell and the lake of fire after physical death. This is considered the second death (Revelation 20:6; 20:14; 21:8). Later, in other Scriptures, we find that those in heaven or hell or the lake of fire are conscious of their environments (Matthew 5:29; 13:41-43; Luke 16:23; John 5:29; Revelation 14:9-13; 21:4). The soul is not dead in the sense of unconsciousness or being in a state of nonexistence; rather, the soul lives in a conscious state somewhere forever (Isaiah 66:22-24; Matthew 9:44- 48). If one's soul is found in heaven, then one is in a state of blessed consciousness. If one finds himself in hell—or after the final judgment of God, in the lake of fire—then one is in a final state of conscious punishment, and is seen spiritually as a second death: a state of conscious, painful separation from God—the creator of all things.

To sum up this part of our discussion, we need to remember the major concept of our soul and spirit being made in the metaphysical likeness of God—this concept is critically important when we begin to talk in our next chapter about Jesus Christ, the Son of God, taking on human flesh and living among us (John 1:1, 14).

MANKIND IN THE IMAGE OF GOD

When we speak of "likeness," we are speaking of the metaphysical makeup of God and Mankind. When we speak of "image," we are speaking of something else. Why do I think this? Many theologians believe that the terms "image" and "likeness" used in Genesis 1:26 are parallel terms; that is, they are terms being used to say the same thing for emphasizing a point being made. This is how some of the language is constructed in what we call the "poetic books" or "the writings," which are part of the Scripture, and is used as a teaching method format. We find this format in books such as Psalms, Proverbs, Song of Solomon, Job and Ecclesiastes. But Genesis is not a book that lends itself to this type of format. Genesis is part of the "Pentateuch" or the books of "the Law"—which comprise the first five books of the Scriptures—and tends to be more technical in nature. Although you will find some poetic forms of writing within these books, it is limited in comparison to the poetic books.

If we follow the normal grammatical sentence structure of the English language, when God states, "Let us make man in Our image, according to Our likeness," we should understand the key phrase to be "according to," which is a preposition preceding the noun "likeness." The word "according" is a technical term meaning to be consistent with, or to be in harmony with, some known pattern. The image being spoken of must be consistent with, or in harmony with, God's pattern or metaphysical structure. Therefore, if we understand God's metaphysical structure as we have presented it in this book, then "God's image" must refer to attributes of that structure. If we understand these two concepts in this light, then "image" and "likeness" are not a parallelism. Allow me to illustrate this. If I had a car and said to you, "Let's make a different car in the likeness of this one," how would you understand that? Would the cars physically be and look the same, or would the cars function the same, using the same structural concepts but physically look different? It is my view that being made in God's image means that we are made in God's metaphysical likeness that possess many of God's attributes, but limited by the nature God created us with.

As we stated earlier, God is spirit by nature, giving him unlimited boundaries—whereas mankind is natural (1 Corinthians 15:46); that is, man is made up of body/spirit collectively, which has been stated before. This is the limiting property of mankind: the body/spirit combination.

The Term Parallelism Explained

This section has been added to this revision because there seems to be a need to extend the conversation on the subject matter of Parallelisms. There are those that have argued that there are parallelisms in Genesis to bolster the claims that "soul" and "spirit" is the same thing in parallel form. My response to this argument is as follows.

Parallelism is part of Hebrew poetry—and yes, Hebrew poetry can be found in other parts of the Scriptures besides just in the poetic books, with the book of Genesis as one example. Theologians have for centuries debated the true definition to what parallelism is and how it is used. Robert Lowth, in the 18th century, proposed three kinds of parallelism: *synonymous*, *antithetic*, and *synthetic*. Although this seems reasonable to many, it has been shown that not all forms of parallelism fit into these categories.[1] As one researches this subject, it would be found that many books have been written on this topic, and therefore it is not my intent to get into a large debate on this whole subject matter. But briefly, allow me to explain my line of reasoning to the conclusions and statements made in the previous section labeled "Mankind in the Image of God."

As one studies this topic of Parallelism, two elements of this topic stand out. One is form, and the other is function. Form consists of language and syntax, which then define "Line," which is the major structural form of Hebrew poetry. This structure can include parallelisms. Because of "Line" structure, Hebrew poetry can be difficult to translate in all cases. Therefore, because of these difficulties there is a debate to how one interprets Genesis 1:27 in light of this structure.

The second element to Hebrew poetry is function. What is the function of this style of language? Its function is to bring the element of personalization to the subject matter, and to evoke some emotional response. Psalms is personalized because it is written in the first person. This places you, the reader, in the forefront. Proverbs evokes personalization through providing wisdom and instruction. Within all this, emotions are evoked as a response to this form of teaching and format.

If you examine Genesis 1:26 and 27, it is my view that neither line form nor the element of emotion is demonstrated to support the argument of parallelism, and therefore should not be viewed as a form of parallelism. Professional translators further support this view by how they structured the syntax in the English translations, as I have expressed in the previous section.

There is a great deal more that could be said, but the purpose of this book is to keep things as simple as possible and try not to complicate the issues at hand in the mind of its readers. And as always, I encourage further study on this issue if it has become an obstacle for your true understanding.

IMAGE OF GOD EXPLORED

We have seen that God and Mankind are metaphysically structured in the same manner. That is, God is made up of both spirit and soul, just as mankind is made up of both spirit and soul. Mankind's spirit functions, in a limited way, in the same fashion as God's: In both cases, the spirit serves as their nature, with similar functionality. Because of this, mankind now has a communications mechanism to God, can reason through a God concept, and in the end, can have a meaningful, conscious relationship with God, the creator of all things. If you think through these concepts, because we are made in God's likeness, we can think, reason, feel emotions and make choices in like manner as the God who created us. We know this to be true even after the fall of mankind, or sin, based on God's confirmation of this analogy through his statement made in Genesis 3:22, when he said: "Behold, the man has become like one of Us, knowing good and evil." Mankind having the ability to have knowledge, and reason through knowledge like God does, is a sign that man is made in a likeness of his creator. This likeness allows us the ability to have a personal and meaningful relationship with the creator, whom we can know and communicate with.

The second aspect to this likeness is God's image, which is reflective of his attributes, such as holiness, goodness, love and so on. These are the attitudes that are the controlling factor of both God and mankind before the fall, or sin.

As we talked about God's attitudes in chapter two, these same attitudes were available in mankind before the fall, and are part of God's image that was imparted to mankind. So how should we view God's image in mankind after the fall? That is a good question, and has been talked about in the theological community for a very long time.

GOD'S IMAGE IN MANKIND AFTER THE FALL OR SIN

There has been a great deal of talk about what happened to mankind after the fall, and how this has affected humanity's image-bearing. As we reviewed the metaphysical structure of mankind in chapters five and six, we began to see the true effects of mankind's fall into sin. As we have made brief mention before, it was mankind's spirit or nature that was corrupted. And because mankind's nature is the controlling factor of both his body and soul, the end effect is that mankind, as a total being, is seen as corrupt before God (Psalm 14:1-3; Psalm 51:1-3; Luke 6:43, KJV). This is why Jesus stated that it is from the heart that corruption originates. This concept also validates the statement found in Proverbs 23:7, which say, "For as he thinketh in his heart, so is he" (KJV). Thus, it is our attitudes that originate within our spirit, which guide us in everyday life.

In reality, mankind is still metaphysically in God's likeness, but God's image in mankind has been altered by sin. We can no longer duplicate or reflect God's attitudes as we once could do. That is, we can no longer be holy as God is holy. Our morality has been altered and no longer has the capability to duplicate or reflect God's image. So what is the answer? Can this image be repaired or made whole again? The answer is, YES! Mankind can be made into a new creature in Christ Jesus (2 Corinthians 5:17), and the image mankind once displayed can be restored once again. Why? Because we were made in God's likeness, which was never altered by sin. What was altered? Our reflection of God's moral attributes through the corruption of our nature by sin. By God giving us a new nature, through the sacrificial work of Christ (Ephesians 2:1-22), we can once again reflect God's image in an intermittent way. What do I mean by "intermittent"? Let us talk about that.

The born-again believer in Christ (1 Peter 1:23) has two natures, as we have discussed in previous chapters; this means that there is a battle waging in our souls between these two natures (Romans 7:14-25). When we choose to follow the attitudes of the new nature, then we truly reflect God's image, but when we choose to follow the attitudes of our old nature, then we do not reflect God's image. In either scenario, we will always be in God's likeness, but his true image can only be displayed when we submit our wills to God through our new nature (Colossians 2:9-11). It should be noted that when regenerated mankind is resurrected from the dead, they will all be in a permanent state of being in God's uncorrupted image again (1 Peter 1:3-9; 1 Corinthians 15:49-58).

CLOSING COMMENTS

It is at this point that I feel the need to make another comment concerning the nature of this book. It is not my intent to limit the importance of the sacrifice of Jesus Christ in this chapter concerning salvation or image bearing. It is my intent to follow the theme of this book in the area of the nature of things, thus showing how all of God collectively is working in the world for his glory, while at the same time helping us understand God, mankind, and the nature of things.

Now that we have added another chapter to our knowledge base, let us move on to chapter eight as we apply these concepts, along with others discussed in previous chapters, to the person and work of Jesus Christ the God/Man.

PART THREE: MANKIND MADE IN THE IMAGE OF GOD | 151

Chapter Seven Endnotes

---

[1] http://www.oxfordbiblicalstudies.com/resource/lessonplan_15.xhtml (Link noted as source of information.)

Chapter Eight

JESUS CHRIST BOTH GOD AND MAN

As we move into this chapter, it is not my intent to represent Jesus Christ as anything less than God, or to take away the majesty or authority that Father has bestowed upon him. It is my intent to demonstrate in a metaphysical way how Jesus can be God and still take on the form of a man as the Scriptures have declared (Philippians 2:6-7).

JESUS AS GOD

The person of Jesus Christ is a complicated one, because of the claims he makes concerning himself throughout the Gospels, which are the only biographical historical accounts we have of his life while living among us. But before we look at this part of our knowledge base, let us see if we can find anything in the Old Testament that may provide some additional insight into his origin.

The Scriptures teach that Jesus Christ is God incarnate—that is, Jesus, God's only Son by nature, came to earth and took on flesh through a virgin's birth, which was produced by the Holy Spirit of God and the Virgin Mary. Mary then became the wife of Joseph, a descendent of King David. Jesus Christ, besides coming to be the savior of the world (1 John 4:14), was also given three additional roles in Scripture, which are Prophet, Priest and King. All of these facts can be verified as we compare God's revelation given in both the Old and New Testaments.

Our discussion in the last chapter showed God making the following statement in Genesis 1:26: "Let Us make man in Our image." The usage of "Us" and "Our" are plural terms and historically have been understood to mean that within the single essence of God there is more than one person that makes up God—and as we have discussed in past chapters, we have established that there are actually three persons in the Godhead: God the Father, God the Son and God the Holy Spirit. We also know from past discussions that God the Father is the plan maker and has established his plans for redeeming his creation from its fall into sin. This plan is revealed to us through God's covenants, or promises, as made to Abraham, King David and the nation Israel.

As we progress into this chapter, we will see that it is the person of Jesus Christ that becomes God's WORD in living flesh to fulfill these promises (John 1:1, 14). Let us walk through the Scriptures and see how all this falls into place.

Within previous discussions, we have learned that Genesis 12:1-3 and 17:1-8 speak of the Abrahamic covenant, which states that God will establish a great nation through Abraham and Sarah, and that this nation will have land that will belong to them forever. As a result of this blessing and promise, God will also bless all nations in the future. What is the blessing that all nations will receive? The answer comes to us in Acts 3:25, along with Galatians 3:8-9, which states: "And the Scripture, foreseeing that God would justify the Gentiles by faith, preached the gospel beforehand to Abraham, saying, 'All the nations shall be blessed in you.' So then those who are of faith are blessed with Abraham, the believer." Moreover, what is this gospel preached beforehand? The Gospel is the good news that Jesus would take on flesh (John 1:1, 14), and become the sacrificial lamb that will take away the sins of the world, through his death, burial, and bodily resurrection (1 Corinthians 15:1-8; Romans 1:16-17; Matthew 4:23; John 1:29; Isaiah 53:3-6). This message was also proclaimed by the angel of the Lord in Luke 2:10-11 as he stated: "Do not be afraid; for behold, I bring you good news of a great joy which shall be for all the people; for today in the city of David there has been born for you a Savior, who is Christ the Lord."

After the establishment of Abraham's blood line (Matthew 1:1-17), along with the land God gave him (Psalm 105:6-12; Numbers 34:1-12), we come to a second covenant called the Davidic covenant, which is a promise that King David's throne will be established forever (2 Samuel 7:14-17). How will this be accomplished? It will be through the establishment of God's kingdom with Jesus Christ as the final and eternal King (Micah 5:2; Matthew 2:5-6; 4:17).

The last covenant put in place by God was the New Covenant. Jeremiah 31:31-34 sets up the permanent indwelling of the person of the Holy Spirit and the permanent forgiveness of mankind's sins. And how shall all this get fulfilled? All unconditional covenants are fulfilled through the earthly life, death and bodily resurrection of Jesus Christ. Let us walk through some Scriptures to validate these claims.

Deuteronomy 18:18-20 speaks to the fact of God sending a prophet, in the future, that would proclaim all that God wants us to know pertaining to part of Abraham's covenant, as spoken of in Genesis 12:3 and represented in the Gospels. This interpretation is confirmed for us in Acts 3:18-26, as it states that Jesus is the prophet promised to convey God's message of salvation to the world. This same message was also proclaimed through other prophecies such as Psalm 2:7 and confirmed in Acts 13:26-39. There are other prophecies concerning Jesus being priest forever and seated at the right hand of the God the Father to be the judge of the nations, as found in Psalms 110, with interpretations confirmed for us in Matthew 22:44; Mark 12:36; Luke 20:42; Acts 2:33-34; and Hebrews 6:20 and 7:17. And finally, the prophecy conveying God's appointed king to his eternal Kingdom is found in Zechariah 9:9 and confirmed for us in Matthew 21:4-10 and John 12:14-16. There are hundreds of prophecies in Scripture pertaining to the coming, ruling and reigning of Jesus Christ. These prophecies spoke to Jesus' incarnation as well as his second coming in the future.

With the Scriptures referenced here, we have confirmed the role of Christ as Prophet, Priest and King. From this point, we will now move on to the issue of Jesus Christ being both God and Man.

JESUS BECOMING MAN

To help us understand the phenomenon of God taking on flesh, we need to be reminded of some concepts already presented.

As seen in chapter seven, we know that mankind is made in the likeness of God. Therefore, the metaphysical makeup of soul and spirit for Jesus as God and for mankind are the same in purpose and function. It is my belief that the makeup of soul and spirit in God and mankind are also made of the same substance, humanly speaking, as discussed in our last chapter. Because of this, Jesus taking on flesh would not be any problem, as mankind was already made in his image according to God's likeness. For Jesus to plug his soul and spirit into a human body would only limit some of his abilities as God, such as being subjected to the five senses of the human body, producing the ability to feel physical pain, to become physically hungry or thirsty, to become physically tired—and for the first time, due to his human nature, be tempted as we are tempted—and experience physical death, none of which had any effect on his God nature. Let us review these concepts and see what we can understand according to our knowledge base.

We know from past discussions that the human body and "matter" are not evil, so for Jesus to take on a human body would not present any problems for him as God. We also know according to Scripture that when Jesus took on flesh, two things took place: First, he became a life form a little lower than the angels (Psalm 8:5; Hebrews 2:7-9), and secondly, he took on a sinless human nature (2 Corinthians 5:16-21; Romans 1:3 NIV). So what does this all mean? To help us understand this in a visual way, allow me to present to you figure 8.1 that follows.

If mankind is made in God's likeness, and is designed to reflect God's image, then metaphysically Jesus as God could infuse himself into a human body without any dysfunction. By such action, Jesus remains God, because as I stated before in chapter two, any person inside the circle called the spirit of God is God, just as figure 8.1 illustrates. Jesus is also metaphysically man because he has taken on human nature in the body/spirit combination. In the end, what we see in figure 8.1 is that Jesus Christ is fully God and fully Man by nature, just as the Scriptures teach and the Christian church has held to from the beginning of the first century, and reaffirmed to us by the Christian church councils in the fourth century. All this is to say that this model does not contradict the Nicene Creed of 325 or 381 A.D., but instead explains why the statements of that Creed are true.

The Apostle Paul supports this assessment as he writes in Romans 1:1-4:

> Paul, a servant of Christ Jesus, called to be an apostle and set apart for the gospel of God—the gospel he promised beforehand through his prophets in the Holy Scriptures regarding his Son, who as to his human nature was a descendant of David, and who through the Spirit of holiness was declared with power to be the Son of God by his resurrection from the dead: Jesus Christ our Lord. (NIV)

The "Spirit of holiness" spoken of in this passage is the same as the "spirit of God" or God's nature, which is holy and is where God's power resides. Thus, Paul is affirming for us that Jesus was both God by nature and Man by nature. The proof of Jesus Christ being God by nature was demonstrated for us in his resurrection from the dead as declared for us here in this passage.

From here, we want to look at some Scriptures to see how all this came to be, and how it all works in reality, which is the true nature of things.

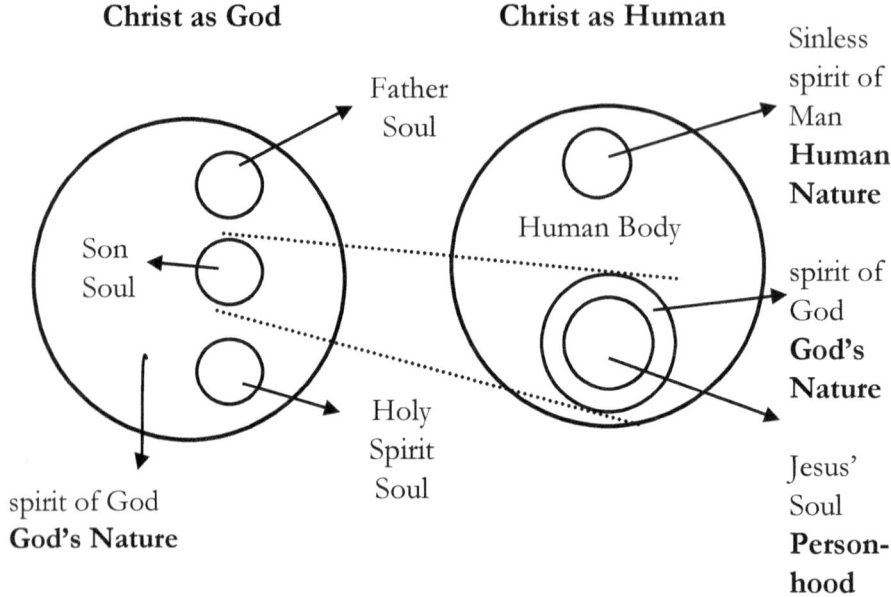

The Metaphysical Makeup of Christ in Human Form
Figure 8.1

Jesus and the Birth Process

We are told in Isaiah 7:14 the following: "Therefore the Lord himself shall give you a sign; Behold, a virgin shall conceive, and bear a son, and shall call his name Immanuel." Approximately 700 years later, an angel of the Lord came to Mary first, then to Joseph, and announced the fulfillment of Isaiah's prophesies as confirmed for us in Matthew 1:18-25 and Luke 1:26-38.

It was through this birth process that Jesus was infused into human flesh. What can this tell us about human nature? It tells us that mankind's sinful nature is passed on through the male. Mary was not pregnant by Joseph, but by the Holy Spirit. This allowed Jesus' human nature to be like Adam's before the fall or sin—thus Jesus became the second Adam, as the Scriptures state in First Corinthians 15:45-49:

So also it is written, "The first man, Adam, became a living soul." The last Adam became a life-giving spirit. However, the spiritual is not first, but the natural; then the spiritual. The first man is from the earth, earthy; the second man is from heaven. As is the earthy, so also are those who are earthy; and as is the heavenly, so also are those who are heavenly. And just as we have borne the image of the earthy, we shall also bear the image of the heavenly.

Romans 5:14 brings confirmation to this issue by telling us that through Adam, or the male, our sin nature is passed on to all mankind, and that Adam served as a "type" of the one to come, which was Jesus Christ. A "type" is a representation or model of some concept to be presented in the future. Adam was a model through metaphysical likeness to what Christ would be like. Christ came in the likeness of Adam's human structure and nature to show us that Adam sinned by choice, not by design. The metaphysical structure of Adam was the same as Christ's, with the exception that Adam did not have two natures, but only one.

The Effects of the Human Body on Christ

Chapter two and three's discussion on God's spirit and soul told us that God functions similarly to mankind's soul and spirit, as discussed in chapters five and six. Because of these similarities, when Jesus infused himself into a human body, his personhood became subjected to the limitation of that body. Just what those limitations were, is a matter of interpretation. It is my view that the major limitations were that for the first time, God could experience mankind's physical pain, thirstiness, temptation and physical death. This is all significant, because before this time, God never could experience such things like humans could, nor did he ever need to. There are many questions that arise from this scenario, so let us look at some of these issues.

The Temptation of Christ

The Scriptures record for us the account of Christ's temptation in Luke 4:1-13, which reads as follows:

> And Jesus, full of the Holy Spirit, returned from the Jordan and was led about by the Spirit in the wilderness for forty days, being tempted by the devil. And He ate nothing during those days; and when they had ended, He became hungry. And the devil said to Him, "If You are the Son of God, tell this stone to become bread." And Jesus answered him, "It is written, 'Man shall not live on bread alone.'" And he led Him up and showed Him all the kingdoms of the world in a moment of time. And the devil said to Him, "I will give You all this domain and its glory; for it has been handed over to me, and I give it to whomever I wish. Therefore if You worship before me, it shall all be Yours." And Jesus answered and said to him, "It is written, 'You shall worship the Lord your God and serve Him only.'" And he led Him to Jerusalem and had Him stand on the pinnacle of the temple, and said to Him, "If You are the Son of God, throw Yourself down from here; for it is written, 'He will give His angels charge concerning You to guard You,' and, 'On their hands they will bear You up, Lest You strike Your foot against a stone.'" And Jesus answered and said to him, "It is said, 'You shall not put the Lord your God to the test.'"
>
> And when the devil had finished every temptation, he departed from Him until an opportune time.

James 1:13 states, that God cannot be tempted by evil. So how does that play out here with Christ being tempted by evil? The answer lies with the metaphysical makeup of Jesus Christ. Jesus as God could not be tempted. However, Jesus, subjected to a second human nature, could. This was the purpose of the temptation—to demonstrate that Eve's sin was by choice and not by some flaw in God's metaphysical design. Eve did not eat the fruit because she was hungry, but because it was pleasing to the eye to look at, and because of Satan's suggestion that if she ate the fruit, she would become wise like God. Because of these two factors, she chose to disobey God; thus, sin befell mankind. Jesus' temptation duplicated this scenario and showed mankind that Eve's choice was preventable. Jesus duplicated and maximized the event by first fasting for 40 days and becoming hungry before the temptation. Eve was not hungry when she gave in. Second, Jesus was tempted by three different offers; one only tempted Eve. In the end, the event that caused Eve to sin was duplicated and amplified for the purpose of showing that sin, for mankind, was a choice and not a design flaw on God's part. James goes on in his statement saying that not only can God not be tempted, but also God tempts no one. This statement reinforces the fact that it was Satan that tempted humanity—not God!

At this point, for many, this discussion leads us into the sovereignty and foreknowledge of God. But because of the immense depth to these topics and their implications within theology, I will hold our discussion in balance to the focus of this book. Therefore, I will only touch briefly on these two topics in order to provide food for thought and encourage you to study these topics through their own Scriptural merits.

As you research these two topics, you will find that the theology behind the topics of sovereignty and foreknowledge are sometime expanded through philosophical thought and could lead to a misunderstanding of the true nature and meaning behind these two subjects. Again, it is always good to remember that for biblical truth to be true, it must agree with all other biblical truth. With this in mind, let us look briefly at these two topics and then move on.

The Sovereignty of God

Sovereignty simply means to have supreme power and authority over something or have complete freedom to do, without any external influence. Example: If I worked thirty years at a job and through my paychecks purchased some property free of any loans, liens or taxes, you could say I have sovereign power over that property. I have earned the right to have the freedom to control that property without any outside influence—I have sovereignty over it.

Now let us up size the example. Think of the universe as property. "In the beginning God made the heavens and the earth" (Genesis 1:1). Because God is the property owner of everything in existence without any debts owed—God is then sovereign or holds sovereignty over everything just as the Scriptures state: "The Lord has established His throne in the heavens; And His sovereignty rules over all." (Psalm 103:19)

The Scriptures provide a few examples to help us understand this concept from God's perspective. Consider the following conversational examples, which read: "You turn things around! Shall the potter be considered as equal with the clay, That what is made should say to its maker, 'He did not make me'; Or what is formed say to him who formed it, 'He has no understanding'"? (Isaiah 29:16) Or, "On the contrary, who are you, O man, who answers back to God? The thing molded will not say to the molder, "Why did you make me like this," will it? Or does not the potter have a right over the clay, to make from the same lump one vessel for honorable use, and another for common use?" (Romans 9:20-21) Then there is this perspective:

> Then the Lord answered Job out of the whirlwind and said, Who is this that darkens counsel By words without knowledge? Now gird up your loins like a man, And I will ask you, and you instruct Me! Where were you when I laid the foundation of the earth? Tell Me, if you have understanding, Who set its measurements, since you know? Or who stretched the line on it? On what were its bases sunk? Or who laid its cornerstone, When the morning stars sang together, And all the sons of God shouted for joy? Or who enclosed the sea with doors, When, bursting forth, it went out from the womb; When I made a cloud its garment, And thick darkness its swaddling band, And I placed boundaries on it, And I set a bolt and doors, And I said, 'Thus far you shall come, but no farther; And here shall your proud waves stop'? Have you ever in your life commanded the morning, And caused the dawn to know its place; That it might take hold of the ends of the earth, And the wicked be shaken out of it? It is changed like clay under the seal; And they stand forth like a garment. And from the wicked their light is withheld, And the uplifted arm is broken. Have you entered into the springs of the sea? Or have you walked in the recesses of the deep? Have the gates of death been revealed to you? Or have you seen the gates of deep darkness? Have you understood the expanse of the earth? Tell Me, if you know all this. (Job 38:1-18)

This conversation continues as we read:

> Then the Lord said to Job, Will the faultfinder contend with the Almighty? Let him who reproves God answer it. Then Job answered the Lord and said, Behold, I am insignificant; what can I reply to Thee? I lay my hand on my mouth. Once I have spoken, and I will not answer; Even twice, and I will add no more.
> Then the Lord answered Job out of the storm, and said, Now gird up your loins like a man; I will ask you, and you instruct Me. Will you really annul My judgment? Will you condemn Me that you may be justified? Or do you have an arm like God, And can you thunder with a voice like His? Adorn yourself with eminence and dignity; And clothe yourself with honor and majesty. Pour out the overflowings of your anger; And look on everyone who is proud, and make him low. Look on everyone who is proud, and humble him; And tread down the wicked where they stand. Hide them in the dust together; Bind them in the hidden place. Then I will also confess to you, That your own right hand can save you. (Job 40:1-14)

These are revelational examples of how God defines and sees his sovereignty. Our understanding of this concept becomes problematic in our minds when we see ourselves as sovereign beings, displaying attitudes of: I did that, I made that, I worked for that! No one helped me accomplish that; I did this on my own; accompanied with possession attitudes such as: those are my children; that is my house, my car, my job. From the time we are born to the time we die, many of us are led to believe we are the starting point to our existence, as if our parents, family or friends had no influence on our existence and we are beholden to no one. It is true that at some point humans do exert efforts to build for themselves a life and the feelings of sovereignty do come, but in reality it is my view that no human being is ever entirely sovereign over their own life. Humans have been given rights by God, such as the right to life until God takes it back or one forfeits it under God's law. (This is why we should value life; it is God-given worth to humanity.) Another God-given right is free will or the right of choice, within the boundaries of current human nature. Why? Because it's part of being made in the likeness of God! The ability to reason and make choices is God-given, and one reason why God made us to be in his image—to be free agents. And with choice comes responsibility for oneself, for the Scriptures teach that we will always reap what we have sown—good or bad. There are other privileges that may sometimes be given to us by God and others, but in reality, no human being holds true sovereignty over themselves. We are all subject to some higher God-given authority, such as the triune God, a marriage relationship, governments we find ourselves living under, or the Church we are members of; this is something to think about! (Genesis 2:24; 1 Corinthians 7:1-5; Numbers 11:16-17; Deuteronomy 1:9-17, 17:8-13; Romans 13:1-7; Ephesians 4: 11-12; 1 Timothy 3:1-13; 1 Peter 5:1-5)

My comments here are not meant to be political in nature; I am simply pointing out the fact that true sovereignty is God's alone to claim—and everything else, including authority, is granted by God within his creation.

The Foreknowledge of God

The foreknowledge of God is spoken of theologically as well as philosophically. Let us briefly look at this subject to see if we can bring better understanding.

Foreknowledge simply means to know something before it is going to happen. When we speak about the foreknowledge of God, the question becomes, How does God know anything before it is going to happen? The answer comes in our understanding of the concept of time. With God, there is no element of time. God lives and functions outside the dimensions of time. How should we understand this? Time, along with everything else, is a created piece of our natural universe. It is part of our natural laws that govern our universe, as we understand it. Remember those math story problems that asked, if something was travelling this fast, and it was this many miles away from point "A", how much time would it take to get there? Well, in science, time becomes an important factor. It provides us with some sense of relativity. Why is this important? Because the world and all of humanity had a starting point; and from that point, we as humans make reference in time to keep track of the past, present and future. Our math formulas, primarily in the world of physics, have built into them a reference of time; without it, we would not be able to solve many problems. Example: Without the reference of time, we would not be able to calculate the speed of light or the frequency of any wavelength.

In contrast, God is eternal—without beginning or ending—time is not required for God to function or exist. Remember Albert Einstein's discovery that matter and energy are relative as represented in the math formula: $E = Mc^2$. This discovery has revealed that the constant in our universe is not time, but the speed of light (c). The constants of time can change in our universe based on the gravity of mass, but the speed of light never changes; it is not affected by gravity like time is. Therefore, since God is the creator of the universe's light source (Genesis 1:3), it is only logical to believe that God can and does function outside the box of time. He can see everything before, during and after any given event inside the box of time he created. To help visualize this, think of being in outer space and looking at the earth, as seen in pictures taken from spacecraft. We see the earth as a whole planet, with all the black space surrounding it. Now think of the surrounding blackness as outside of time. Time has no effect on that space. Then think of the earth as totally dependent on time. Everything that happens on earth—happens with time as a factor. The blackness does not care about time. It will go and go and go—without ending. But the earth operates by a clock. It has a starting point and, without God's intervention, an ending point. This is what time is—a restrictive scientific rule that governs everything that is tied to it.

Therefore, God standing outside the box can see the whole picture like a movie, because he is not governed or restricted by time, as someone pointed out to me—God is bigger than time. This then leads us into a discussion to how God operates and plans events within that box of time, which then moves us into a whole new discussion on the planning and execution of the will of God for his creation based on his rights of sovereignty. To speak to this topic would be to speak to the subject of motive. The Scriptures state in First Corinthians 2:11: "For who among men knows the thoughts of a man except the spirit of the man, which is in him? Even so the thoughts of God no one knows except the Spirit of God." This means no one knows the motives or plans of God without God revealing them to us, which in some cases he does and in others, he does not. The hidden motives of God lead us to speculation, a practice in theology we are warned to avoid (1 Timothy 1:3-7).

So then, to stay the course of this study, we must stay on the subject at hand and finish our discussion on the metaphysical make up of Jesus Christ as God and Man and the nature of things.

The Miracles of Christ

As we look at Jesus' miracles, we see that being in a human body did not prevent him from using his God nature to demonstrate power, omniscience or authority as God.

This is demonstrated in the following passages: Matthew 14:24-28 states that Jesus walked on the sea or water. This demonstrates that Jesus as God had control of the elements. Matthew 8:5-13 is an illustration that Jesus could control the healing process without even being in the presence of the patient. Matthew 12:22-28 states that Jesus has authority to cast out demons, and that this was done by the power of the spirit of God. It is this passage that tells us that it was Jesus' nature as God that demonstrated the power required to command other spirits.

The Limitations of Christ

The only real limitation I see Jesus having was that he could not leave his human body like demons could—short of death. Jesus had to die to change back to what he was before his incarnation—an unlimited state of being. How do we know this? Jesus tells us in John 14:3: "And if I go and prepare a place for you, I will come back and take you to be with me that you also may be where I am." (NIV) Jesus was referring to his ascension as mentioned in Acts chapter one. This concept, tied to our past discussion on the purpose of spiritual bodies, shows that until Jesus died, he was infused into a human form. This also demonstrates that Jesus did not possess a human body in a similar manner as the demon possession concept. Jesus became flesh and infused himself into the human body and nature, making him subject to the five senses of the body. But because Jesus had his God nature as well, he also could exercise supernatural abilities such as knowing the thoughts of others (Luke 6:8; John 2:24), healing every kind of affliction (Matthew 4:24; 8:16; Mark 1:34; Luke 5:15), and controlling nature's elements (Luke 5:4-8; Matthew 14:25; Mark 4:39). It is interesting to note that even though Jesus was in a human body, he still could do supernatural things within that body. All of it could be attributed to his spirit or nature's attributes as discussed in chapter two. If you examine figure 8.1, many of the questions of how Jesus can be or do something is answered by the metaphysical description and makeup of the God/Man, Jesus Christ.

THE TRANSFER OF POWER

Questions may arise as to the miracles the Apostles performed during and after Christ's life on earth, such as raising the dead, healing the sick, making the blind see again, and so on. Is it possible for mortals to perform such things? Metaphysically speaking, the answer is yes. If you review figure 6.2 in chapter six, you would see that this type of power comes from the function of the spirit of God, which acts as the born-again believer's new nature.

If this is true, then why do we not see this type of healing today? The answer to that question is complicated. But let us see if we can bring some common sense discussion to this issue.

The type of power required to perform such healing can only come from the supernatural world of God. How do we know this? We know this through two observations. First, Exodus 4:11 states: "And the Lord said to him, 'Who has made man's mouth? Or who makes him dumb or deaf, or seeing or blind? Is it not I, the Lord?'" In context, this statement is in reference to God influencing the human birth process. If God is the author of such things in this process, would he then not be the source for healing as reasoned in John 9:1-3 which states: "As he went along, he saw a man blind from birth. His disciples asked him, 'Rabbi, who sinned, this man or his parents, that he was born blind?' 'Neither this man nor his parents sinned,' said Jesus, 'but this happened so that the work of God might be displayed in his life.'" (NIV)

Secondly, when the Pharisees accused Jesus of healing and casting out demons by the power of Satan, Jesus responded with the following logic:

> Then there was brought to Him a demon possessed man who was blind and dumb, and He healed him, so that the dumb man spoke and saw. And all the multitudes were amazed, and began to say, "This man cannot be the Son of David, can he?" But when the Pharisees heard it, they said, "This man casts out demons only by Beelzebul the ruler of the demons." And knowing their thoughts He said to them, "Any kingdom divided against itself is laid waste; and any city or house divided against itself shall not stand. And if Satan casts out Satan, he is divided against himself; how then shall his kingdom stand? And if I by Beelzebul cast out demons, by whom do your sons cast them out? Consequently they shall be your judges. But if I cast out demons by the Spirit of God, then the kingdom of God has come upon you. Or how can anyone enter the strong man's house and carry off his property, unless he first binds the strong man? And then he will plunder his house." (Matthew 12:22-29)

If we examine these passages, we can conclude that mankind's suffering comes to us through our sin, or by the acts of Satan or God for reasons known only to God. In the end, the true healer in all cases is God; for Satan is not out to free us, but to destroy us as First Peter 5:8 and Romans 6:23 proclaim. We also see these concepts demonstrated to us in the book of Job of the Old Testament, where Satan, with God's permission, inflicted death and pain, but it was only God who restored.

Another element of the availability of this power is that it is not for purchase or sale. How do we know this? Acts 8:18-24 tells us the story of Simon trying to purchase the power of the Holy Spirit and was rebuked and told to repent of such thoughts. This concept was expanded when the Apostles where given instruction by Christ not to take anything with them, including money, as they went out to proclaim the Gospel message and perform healing miracles (Luke 9:1-6).

We also know that the power of the Holy Spirit is part of all born-again believers in Jesus Christ. We know this by the very metaphysical structure as shown in figure 6.2. But how that power is accessed is the key to its display in the world. The Scriptures speak to the spiritual gift of healing. Some believe this gift still exists today; some do not (1

Corinthians 12:9). Some believe it is just a matter of having enough faith, others believe it all depends on the will of God alone. In the end, it is not a matter of what you or I believe; it is what the Scriptures teach collectively. We are taught in Scripture several principles concerning healing, and if we balance all the concepts out, we will have some understanding of the reality of and access to God's power. To wade through all the different teachings and principles would take another book and is not the focus of this one, so let me provide a few concepts for thought and then move on.

The Scriptures teach us in John 9:1-3 that God sometimes heals for the sole purpose to bring himself glory and honor. In Matthew 15:24-28, we find that healing took place strictly based on one's faith and persistence in asking. In Luke 17:13-19 and Romans 9:15, we learn that healing comes strictly by the mercy of God. The Apostle Paul asked healing for himself three times, but God chose not to grant his request, but instead told him: "my grace is sufficient for you." Within all this, we are told that we have not because we ask not. And when we do ask, we ask for all the wrong reasons (James 4:1-10). Is the power of God available today for healing? Absolutely! And God heals people every day. Does he always get the glory or credit? No! But the physical healing of God goes on all the same, because God is a loving and merciful God (Jonah 4:2). Does God heal through the so-called great faith healers we see on TV? Based on these principles, it is my opinion that he is not working, in many of those situations, to the extent many believe him to be. Why? Because from my perspective, I believe that in many cases money, pride or arrogance is riding in the background at such events—and as we can see in Scripture, God opposes the proud and removes his blessing on those that would try to profit from the free and merciful power of God (Isaiah 2:11-12; James 4:6; 1 Peter 5:5). And remember, being financially prosperous does not always represent God's blessing (1 Corinthians 4:9-13). So it is; healing comes by the power of God according to his perfect and sovereign will (2 Corinthians 12:8-9). It is my practice to apply the whole counsel of God through faith, practice and prayer, and leave the rest up to God to work out his perfect will for his own (Romans 8:26-28).

Conclusion of this Section

The purpose of this section was to demonstrate that God's power is real and available through the new nature of all believers, both by the promise of God and by the metaphysical structure of mankind in a regenerated state. This discussion took place here because we needed to understand that God's power was not just available to Jesus Christ and his disciples, but to all those that are part of God's adopted family and have been grafted into God's nature, the true source of this power. As Jesus stated in John 10:24-25, the purpose for all his miracles was to prove who he claimed to be, the incarnate Son of God; this is supported through the statements of the Apostle John as he wrote:

> Jesus said to him, "Because you have seen Me, have you believed? Blessed are they who did not see, and yet believed."
> Many other signs therefore Jesus also performed in the presence of the disciples, which are not written in this book; but these have been written that you may believe that Jesus is the Christ, the Son of God; and that believing you may have life in His name. (John 20:29-31)

THE PURPOSE FOR THE DUAL NATURE OF CHRIST

We now come to an important issue, and one that has eluded me for many years. Why? It is because mankind's nature and God's nature function in similar fashion and share similar purposes. For this reason my question has been, why would Jesus need a human spirit to function as a human? Could not Jesus just plug in his soul and spirit into a human body and function as a human?

It is my view that Jesus could have done just that, and no one would have known any differently. Jesus' soul and spirit could have been infused through the virgin birth into the human body and caused it to function just as it functions now. Jesus would have demonstrated emotion, intellect and will, along with being sinless, feeling pain, getting thirsty and bleeding; and the body would still have been required to die in order for him to exit the human body with all its limitations. All this could have taken place because we are made in God's likeness metaphysically. This scenario has always been my dilemma. So what is the answer?

If the human spirit was not part of the metaphysical makeup of Christ, then the Scriptures would be incorrect to label Christ as the second Adam (1 Corinthians 15:45-47) or make the statement, "One who has been tempted in all things as we are, yet without sin." (Hebrews 4:15) This would mean God lied. A second issue lies with the reason for the temptation. The purpose of the temptation was to demonstrate that Eve's sin was a choice, not a programmed design response, which speaks to the issue of Eve having free will before the fall or sin.

All of this is very interesting, which leads us back to the discussion of chapter six. After Christ's death and resurrection, does Christ need a human nature? It is my view that he does not, for similar reasons as I expressed in chapter six. Jesus was resurrected with a glorified body, which looks human, but the need for a human spirit is no longer required. All Scriptures are fulfilled concerning the resurrected Christ, and therefore, Jesus is free to be as he always was—God—only remaining in human form, a form that was not unfamiliar to Christ before his incarnation. This observation comes from the account recorded for us in the book of Daniel as we read:

> And he commanded certain valiant warriors who were in his army to tie up Shadrach, Meshach and Abed-nego, in order to cast them into the furnace of blazing fire. Then these men were tied up in their trousers, their coats, their caps and their other clothes, and were cast into the midst of the furnace of blazing fire. For this reason, because the king's command was urgent and the furnace had been made extremely hot, the flame of the fire slew those men who carried up Shadrach, Meshach and Abed-nego. But these three men, Shadrach, Meshach and Abed-nego, fell into the midst of the furnace of blazing fire still tied up.
>
> Then Nebuchadnezzar the king was astounded and stood up in haste; he responded and said to his high officials, "Was it not three men we cast bound into the midst of the fire?" They answered and said to the king, "Certainly, O king." He answered and said, "Look! I see four men loosed and walking

about in the midst of the fire without harm, and the appearance of the fourth is like a son of the gods!" Then Nebuchadnezzar came near to the door of the furnace of blazing fire; he responded and said, "Shadrach, Meshach and Abed-nego, come out, you servants of the Most High God, and come here!" Then Shadrach, Meshach and Abed-nego came out of the midst of the fire. And the satraps, the prefects, the governors and the king's high officials gathered around and saw in regard to these men that the fire had no effect on the bodies of these men nor was the hair of their head singed, nor were their trousers damaged, nor had the smell of fire even come upon them. (Daniel 3:20-27)

Bible scholars hold differing opinions to who the fourth figure was in this text. Some hold it to be an angel from God; others interpret it to be literally the Son of God (Jesus Christ). It is my view that the fourth person seen by Nebuchadnezzar represents, what is known in the theological community as, a Christophany. Within modern secular dictionaries, "Christophany" is defined as a manifestation of Christ after his resurrection. This would seem reasonable to most, because Christ was not formally introduced to the world until after his virgin birth. But the Scriptures have always alluded to a coming messiah and the fact that God is represented to be more than one person (Genesis 1:26; Daniel 9:25-26; John 1:41, 4:25). Yet others may see this as a Theophany—a manifestation of God or a deity to humans in a real and metaphysical way. The King James Version of the interlinear Bible translates the phrase "son of the gods" from Hebrew to English like this: "the Son of God." Nebuchadnezzar's comments seem to reflect the image he saw was a deity and not human or an angel.

If we put this event, along with others from the Old Testament, in context of our discussion of the metaphysical make up of Christ, it would seem reasonable to conclude that it is possible that Jesus Christ has always had an eternal presence in some glorified bodily form.

We know of his form because he stated that he would return in the same manner as he left, and that he would be seated on the throne of David forever. This represents a physical presence as expressed in Luke 1:32-33, Revelation 21:3-6 and Acts 1:6-11. The question then comes, did Jesus take on this form at his incarnation or did Jesus always have this form from eternity and therefore will remain in a form he has always possessed? And if this is true, could this not be another aspect of image barring? Something to think about!

JESUS' NATURE IS ETERNAL

Because there is a heresy within the Christian church being propagated and spreading to unsuspecting Christian believers throughout the universal Church, I found it necessary to deal with the question of whether Jesus could lose or give up his deity. This question comes to us because of a false teaching, which believes that when Jesus died on the cross, he gave up his deity at the time of his death, while he spent time suffering in hell for the payment of our sins. This false teaching goes on to say that Jesus regained his deity at the time of his resurrection. Let us look at these issues and see what the Scriptures teach concerning these beliefs.

If Jesus could give up his deity, this would violate two major principles in Scripture: First, the Immutability of God—that is, God's nature can never change; and second that God cannot deny himself (Malachi 3:6; 2 Timothy 2:13). As we stated before in chapter two, when God states that he changes not, he is referring to his nature. Therefore, if Jesus could metaphysically step outside his circle called the "spirit of God," then this would become a change in Christ's or God's nature—making God no longer triune in nature—making the Scripture or God's words null and void. This in essence makes God a liar. Secondly, if Jesus could give up his deity, this would be, in effect, Jesus denying God, and another violation of the Scriptures. That is, God cannot deny himself. Some would argue that the Scriptures stating that God the Father forsaking his Son, while on the cross, (Mark 15:34) is an argument for denial. My response to that argument is, to forsake someone is to turn away from that person, but to deny is to declare untrue. God the Father never denied Jesus to be his only Son.

We come to this issue of deity because of the misunderstanding that Jesus must go to hell and pay for our sins for three days and that somehow this could not be done while still being a deity. It should be noted that there is no place in Scriptures that indicates that this must take place for Christ. The Scriptures teach that the penalty for sin is death. Isaiah 53:12 states: "Because He poured out Himself to death, And was numbered with the transgressors; Yet He Himself bore the sin of many, And interceded for the transgressors." This passage states that it was the physical death process, that Christ subjected himself to, not a spiritual one. This can also be seen in First Peter 2:24-25: "And He Himself bore our sins in His body on the cross, that we might die to sin and live to righteousness; for by His wounds you were healed." Mankind's sins were borne and paid for by the actual crucifixion and physical death of Christ on a Roman cross. If you would like a visual aid to the price Christ actually paid in his crucifixion, I recommend you view Mel Gibson's movie "The Passion of the Christ." Nowhere in Scriptures does it state that Christ spent three days in a physical place called hell and suffered there. If my assessment is true, then what happened during the three days he was in the tomb? That is a good question, and by investigating the Scriptures, we can come to a logical and reasonable conclusion without violating any major doctrinal teaching in the Scriptures.

Ezekiel 26:20 and 32:24 states that there is a place of punishment in the lower parts of the earth. The Scriptures also teach that there is a place called Sheol, which was seen as a place for the dead (Genesis 37:35; Job 11:8; Isaiah 14:9). It is also believed that Sheol, or Hades, was a divided place. In one part there was paradise, as Jesus spoke of in his story of the rich man, and the other part called hell, a place of torment for the wicked—also represented in Jesus' story of the rich man (Luke 16:22-31; Revelation 20:13-14). When the Scriptures speak of this place, it is referred to as where all the dead stayed until the time of Christ's death and resurrection. How do we know Christ went there? Jesus revealed this his destiny as expressed in Matthew 12:40. After Christ's death, we learn the Old Testament saints were taken out of Sheol to heaven. We know this because the Scriptures tell us.

Four Scriptures tell us what happen to Christ during his three days in the tomb. Let us look at them. Psalm 16:10 is a prophecy concerning Christ's death. It is quoted for us again in Acts 2:31-32, which states: "He looked ahead and spoke of the resurrection of the Christ, that He was neither abandoned to Hades, nor did His flesh suffer decay. This

Jesus God raised up again, to which we are all witnesses." Psalm 68:18 is a second prophecy, which is quoted in Ephesians 4:8-10 and states:

Therefore it says,

When He ascended on high,
He led captive a host of captives,
And He gave gifts to men.
Now this expression, "He ascended," what does it
mean except that He also had descended into the lower
parts of the earth? He who descended is Himself also
He who ascended far above all the heavens, that He
might fill all things.

When we put these two concepts together—that Jesus would not be left in Hades, and that he would lead the captives in Hades to ascend on high—we can only conclude that Jesus after his death went to Sheol or Hades to take all the Old Testament saints to heaven with him, then came back to be resurrected. He then walked among mankind only to returned back to his heavenly Father forty days later to be seated on the right hand of God the Father (Ephesians 1:20; Colossians 3:1; Hebrews 1:3; 1 Peter 3:22; Acts 1:3).

To teach in any form that Jesus could give up his deity, at any time, should be seen as heresy and rejected as false teaching. The Scriptures teach that Jesus is God by nature and that his nature is eternal, that is, God's nature has no beginning and no end (Revelation 22:12; Exodus 3:14 KJV). It should also be understood that it would be metaphysically impossible for Christ to separate himself from his God nature; for if this could take place, it would violate what God has said about himself, that God cannot deny himself and God's nature never changes, which would make God out to be a liar. Therefore, the explanation given to what Christ was doing during his three days in the lower parts of the earth is the most consistent with the whole of Scripture. Remember what was said in chapter one? For biblical truth to be true, it must agree with all other biblical truth.

CONCLUSION TO THIS BOOK

Whether or not you accept all or part of the theological concepts or philosophical teaching of this presentation, I challenge you to plug these concepts into all of Scripture and see whether these concepts fit the whole of Scripture; by doing so, it will help you understand God's and Mankind's nature and the source of the nature of things. If you accept any concept presented in this book, and it has helped you to gain a deeper understanding of God or the Scriptures, then I feel I have succeeded in my task to help aid in the edification of the believers in Christ Jesus. It has been my purpose to be accurate and clear in this presentation, and I hope this study has been helpful in aiding you in understanding the nature of God and his working in the world. To concluding this work, I leave you with the Apostle Peter's words as my final thought and summation to this book.

Second Peter 1:2-11 reads:

> Grace and peace be yours in abundance through the knowledge of God and of Jesus our Lord. His divine power has given us everything we need for life and godliness through our knowledge of him who called us by his own glory and goodness. Through these he has given us his very great and precious promises, so that through them you may participate in the divine nature and escape the corruption in the world caused by evil desires. For this very reason, make every effort to add to your faith goodness; and to goodness, knowledge; and to knowledge, self-control; and to self-control, perseverance; and to perseverance, godliness; and to godliness, brotherly kindness; and to brotherly kindness, love. For if you possess these qualities in increasing measure, they will keep you from being ineffective and unproductive in your knowledge of our Lord Jesus Christ. But if anyone does not have them, he is nearsighted and blind, and has forgotten that he has been cleansed from his past sins. Therefore, my brothers, be all the more eager to make your calling and election sure. For if you do these things, you will never fall, and you will receive a rich

welcome into the eternal kingdom of our Lord and Savior Jesus Christ. (NIV)

Because I have spent my life time thinking through these concepts, they seem very clear in my mind, but may not be so clear in yours. Because of this, I leave you the following web link for any questions you may have in working through these concepts. If you benefited from this book, please pass that knowledge on to a friend. In the mean time, I will make every effort, as I have for the past five years, to keep this link working for as long as there is interest, it is technically possible and as it makes sense within my own life's circumstances.

http://booksite.rcetc.com

APPENDICES

EXPLANATION OF APPENDICES

In appendices A and B, you will find all the Scripture references where the word "spirit" appears in the King James Bible (KJV). The KJV was selected for this purpose because thirty-two years ago, when this study was originally started, I only had a full concordance referencing this word in the KJV.

The interpretation of this word, is not limited to the KJV, but was expanded to include six English translations. The Greek text was used to verify that the word "spirit" did appear in the New Testament Scripture, as translated in the English KJV.

In appendices C and D, you will find all the Scriptures referencing the word "Soul" as it appears in the KJV. Again, the interpretation of this word was not limited to the KJV, but was expanded to include six English translations.

Within the KJV, the Greek word used to translate "Holy Ghost" is a different word than that used to translate the word "spirit." The term "Holy Ghost" in the KJV is always used to reference the Holy Spirit and appears about 90 times throughout the New Testament. If you follow this term in the Scriptures, you will find that it falls into the concept of the category listed for Holy Spirit under the Greek word for "spirit"; therefore, there are no contradictions between these terms as expressed in this book.

APPENDIX A

WORD USAGE OF SPIRIT IN THE OLD TESTAMENT

(Listing the Word "SPIRIT" As Referenced in the King James Bible)

OT: RUWACH

APPENDIX KEY:

Scripture references are in **BOLD** font type.
Word Categories are in *ITALICS* font type.
Word usage descriptions are in NORMAL font type.

REFERENCE — *CATEGORY* — USAGE

GENESIS
1:2 — *Spirit of God* — Demonstrating power.
6:3 — *Spirit* — God's nature.
41:8 — *Spirit of Man* — Spirit is troubled because ego is threatened.
41:38 — *Spirit of God* — Associated with wisdom in v39.
45:27 — *Spirit of Man* — Associated with change in attitude or spirit.

EXODUS
6:9 — *Spirit of Man* — Anguish resulting from crushed ego (attitude).
28:3 — *Spirit of Attitude* — Wisdom is an attitude.
31:3 — *Spirit of God* — Associated with wisdom or attitude.
35:21 — *Spirit of Man* — Moved in spirit of attitude.
35:31 — *Spirit of God* — Associated with wisdom or attitude.

NUMBERS
5:14 — *Spirit of Man* — Associated with jealousy (an attitude).
5:30 — *Spirit of Man* — Associated with jealousy (an attitude).
11:17 — *Spirit* — The Holy Spirit.

NUMBERS
11:25 — *Spirit* — The Holy Spirit.
11:25 — *Spirit* — The Holy Spirit.
11:26 — *Spirit* — The Holy Spirit.
11:29 — *Spirit* — The Holy Spirit
14:24 — *Spirit of Attitude* — Had a different attitude from the others.
24:2 — *Spirit* — Caused to speak a discourse.
27:18 — *Spirit of the Lord* — The indwelling of Joshua.

DEUTERONOMY
2:30 — *Spirit of Man* — God caused an effect on man's attitude.
34:9 — *Spirit* — Associated with wisdom. (An attitude).

JOSHUA
5:1 — *Spirit of Attitude* — God caused them to shrink in attitude (pride).

JUDGES
3:10 — *Spirit of the Lord* — The Holy Spirit.
6:34 — *Spirit of the Lord* — The Holy Spirit.
9:23 — *Spirit of Attitude* — God influenced an ill will attitude on people.
11:29 — *Spirit of the Lord* — The Holy Spirit.
13:25 — *Spirit of the Lord* — The Holy Spirit.
14:6 — *Spirit of the Lord* — Holy Spirit providing physical strength.
14:19 — *Spirit of the Lord* — Holy Spirit providing physical strength.
15:14 — *Spirit of the Lord* — Holy Spirit providing physical strength.
15:19 — *Spirit of Man* — Representing his strength of physical life.
16:13 — *Spirit of the Lord* — The Holy Spirit.
16:14 — *Spirit of the Lord* — The Holy Spirit.
16:14 — *Evil Spirit* — From God.

I SAMUEL
1:15 — *Spirit of Man* — Demonstrating an attitude of being wronged
10:6 — *Spirit of the Lord* — Holy Spirit providing the ability of power and change.
10:10 — *Spirit of God* — Provided power to prophesy (communications).
11:6 — *Spirit of God* — God's enabling power.

I Samuel

16:15 — *Evil Spirit* — From God.
16:23 — *Evil Spirit* — From God.
16:23 — *Evil Spirit* — From God.
18:10 — *Evil Spirit* — From God.
19:9 — *Evil Spirit* — From God.
19:20 — *Spirit of God* — Provided power to prophesy (communications).
19:23 — *Spirit of God* — Provided power to prophesy (communications).
30:12 — *Spirit of Man* — Physical strength revived.

II Samuel

23:2 — *Spirit of the Lord* — Holy Spirit spoke.

I Kings

10:5 — *Spirit of Attitude* — An attitude of disbelief.
18:12 — *Spirit of the Lord* The Holy Spirit.
21:5 — *Spirit of Man* — Spirit demonstrating attitude of sadness.
22:21 — *A spirit being* — Influencing man's attitude.
22:22 — *A spirit being* — Influencing man's attitude.
22:23 — *A spirit being* — Influencing man's attitude.
22:24 — *Spirit of the Lord* — The Holy Spirit.

II Kings

2:9 — *Spirit* — A measure of power upon man.
2:15 — *Spirit of the Lord* — The same Holy Spirit on two men.
2:16 — *Spirit of the Lord* — The Holy Spirit.

I Chronicles

5:26 — *Spirit of Man* — Motivated man to do something.
5:26 — *Spirit of Man* — Motivated man to do something.
12:18 — *Spirit of the Lord* — Spirit came upon him.
28:12 — *Spirit of the Lord* — Spirit conveyed information.

II Chronicles

15:1 — *Spirit of God* — Bringing ability to represent God (wisdom).
18:20 — *Evil Spirit* — Representing a spirit being like an angel.

II Chronicles
18:21 — *Evil Spirit* — Spirit to influence humans in a negative way.
18:22 — *Evil Spirit* — A Spirit being a lying influence.
18:23 — *Spirit of the Lord* — The Holy Spirit.
20:14 — *Spirit of the Lord* — The Holy Spirit speaks.
21:16 — *Spirit of Man* — Spirit of man took on an attitude of ill will.
24:20 — *Spirit of God* — Ability to represent God (wisdom).
36:22 — *Spirit of Man* — Influenced or motivated to do something.

Ezra
1:1 — *Spirit of Man* — Influenced or motivated to do something.
1:5 — *Spirit of Man* — Influenced or motivated to do something.

Nehemiah
9:20 — *Spirit* — The Holy Spirit instructing.
9:30 — *Spirit* — The Holy Spirit testifying against.

Job
4:15 — *Spirit* — Could be an angel or the Holy Spirit speaking.
6:4 — *Spirit of Man* — Speaking of physical life or strength.
7:11 — *Spirit of Man* — Emotion stemming from an attitude.
10:12 — *Spirit of Man* — Reflective of attitude.
15:13 — *Spirit of Man* — Reflective of attitude.
20:3 — *Spirit* — Reflecting wisdom and understanding.
26:4 — *Spirit* — Life.
27:3 — *Spirit of God* — The Holy Spirit controlling the speech.
32:8 — *Spirit of Man* — God gives man understanding.
32:18 — *Spirit* — Attitude or Holy Spirit.
33:4 — *Spirit of God* — Demonstrating power to make.
34:14 — *Spirit of Man* — Man's nature vs. his physical life.

Psalms
31:5 — *Spirit of Man* — Referencing physical life.
32:2 — *Spirit of Man* — Referencing the attitude of deceit.
34:18 — *Spirit of Man* — Referencing an attitude of contriteness.
51:10 — *Spirit of Man* — Referencing a right attitude.

Psalms

51:11 — *Holy Spirit* — The Holy Spirit
51:12 — *Spirit* — Referencing the Holy Spirit in verse 11.
51:17 — *Spirit of Attitude* — Having the right attitude.
76:12 — *Spirit of Man* — The forcing of submission to God (attitude).
77:3 — *Spirit of Man* — A reflection of attitude in memory.
77:6 — *Spirit of Man* — An attitude to search for answers.
78:8 — *Spirit of Man* — Not steadfast based on rebellious attitude.
104:30 — *Spirit* — A demonstration of creative power (Life).
106:33 — *Spirit* — Rebelled against God's authority base on his power.
139:7 — *Spirit* — Demonstrating Omnipresence.
142:3 — *Spirit of Man* — Demonstrating confusion or lack of wisdom.
143:4 — *Spirit of Man* — Demonstrating confusion or lack of wisdom.
143:7 — *Spirit of Man* — Physical strength tied to mental state (man's nature).
143:10 — *Spirit* — Referencing God's nature as good.

Proverbs

1:23 — *Spirit* — Communications to others.
11:13 — *Spirit of Attitude* — An attitude that is faithful in nature.
14:29 — *Spirit of Attitude* — An attitude displaying a lack of patience.
15:4 — *Spirit of Man* — In reference to mental state of mind.
15:13 — *Spirit of Man* — Being influenced by attitude.
16:18 — *Spirit of Attitude* — Haughty.
16:19 — *Spirit of Attitude* — Humbleness.
16:32 — *Spirit of Attitude* — Control of attitude.
17:22 — *Spirit of Attitude* — Understanding spirit from attitude of wisdom.
17:27 — *Spirit of Man* — Referencing mental state of being.
18:14 — *Spirit of Man* — Referencing mental state of being.
18:14 — *Spirit of Man* — Referencing mental state of being.
20:27 — *Spirit of Man* — Mental exercise.
25:28 — *Spirit of Man* — Control over attitudes.
29:23 — *Spirit of Attitude* — Humble in spirit.

ECCLESIASTES

1:14 — *Spirit of Man* — To trouble or vex one's mental state.
1:17 — *Spirit of Man* — To trouble or vex one's mental state.
2:11 — *Spirit of Man* — To trouble or vex one's mental state.
2:17 — *Spirit of Man* — To trouble or vex one's mental state.
2:26 — *Spirit of Man* — To trouble or vex one's mental state.
3:21 — *Spirit of Man* — Human nature
3:21 — *Spirit of Animal* — Animal nature
4:4 — *Spirit of Man* — To trouble or vex one's mental state.
4:6 — *Spirit of Man* — To trouble or vex one's mental state.
4:16 — *Spirit of Man* — To trouble or vex one's mental state.
6:9 — *Spirit of Man* — To trouble or vex one's mental state.
7:8 — *Spirit of Man* — Displaying an attitude of patients.
7:8 — *Spirit of Man* — Displaying an attitude of pride.
7:9 — *Spirit of Man* — Displaying an attitude of hastiness.
8:8 — *Spirit of Man* — Human nature.
8:8 — *Spirit of Man* — Human nature.
10:4 — *Spirit of Man* — Demonstrating anger stemming from an attitude.
11:5 — *Spirit of Man* — Human nature.
12:7 — *Spirit of Man* — Life in the form of human nature.

ISAIAH

4:4 — *Spirit* — Power to judge by the authority of his nature. (Attitude)
4:4 — *Spirit* — Power to purify by the authority of his nature.
11:2 — *Spirit of the Lord* — Holy Spirit brings wisdom and understanding.
11:2 — *Spirit of Attitude* — Wisdom.
11:2 — *Spirit of Attitude* — Wisdom producing understanding.
11:2 — *Spirit of Attitude* — Wisdom producing Knowledge.
19:3 — *Spirit of Attitude* — The attitude or motivation of Egypt.
19:14 — *Spirit of Attitude* — God has influence Egypt's attitude, bring confusion.
26:9 — *Spirit of Man* — Demonstrating an attitude to seek.
28:6 — *Spirit of Attitude* — A source producing attitude and authority to act.
29:4 — *Spirit of Attitude* — A familiarity of one's old nature in general.

Isaiah

29:10 — *Spirit of Attitude* — God brings an attitude that produces lack of wisdom.

29:24 — *Spirit of Attitude* — God brings wisdom to the spirit for understanding.

30:1 — *Spirit* — God's nature or attitudes or way of doing things.

31:3 — *Spirit* — Contrasting physical life vs. spiritual life.

32:15 — *Spirit* — The Holy Spirit.

34:16 — *Spirit* — Collectively as a single being.

38:16 — *Spirit of Man* — Speaking to physical life.

40:7 — *Spirit of the Lord* — The Holy Spirit.

40:13 — *Spirit of the Lord* — Holy Spirit (referenced as He).

42:1 — *Spirit* — Holy Spirit (reference to He).

42:5 — *Spirit* — Life.

44:3 — *Spirit* — God's direct nature influence.

48:16 — *Spirit* — God's power and authority.

54:6 — *Spirit of Man* — Grieving (emotion).

57:15 — *Spirit of Attitude* — Being humble.

57:15 — *Spirit* — A person of humility.

57:16 — *Spirit of Man* — Speaking of mental status.

57:19 — *Spirit of the Lord* — The Holy Spirit.

59:21 — *Spirit Holy* — Spirit as referenced to the New Covenant.

61:1 — *Spirit of the Lord* — The Holy Spirit (set apart, anointed).

61:3 — *Spirit of Attitude* — Attitude of despair.

63:10 — *Holy Spirit* — The Holy Spirit.

63:11 — *Holy Spirit* — The Holy Spirit.

63:14 — *Spirit of the Lord* — The Holy Spirit caused rest.

65:14 — *Spirit of Man* — State of mind (attitude).

66:2 — *Spirit of Man* — Broken pride.

Jeremiah

51:11 — *Spirit of Man* — Moved in motivation (attitude).

Ezekiel

1:12 — *Spirit* — A spirit being (future prophecy).

1:20 — *Spirit* — A spirit being (future prophecy).

EZEKIEL
1:20 — *Spirit* — A spirit being (future prophecy).
1:20 — *Spirit* — A spirit being (future prophecy).
1:21 — *Spirit* — A spirit being (future prophecy).
2:2 — *Spirit* — The Holy Spirit (speaks).
3:12 — *Spirit* — The Holy Spirit.
3:14 — *Spirit* — The Holy Spirit .
3:14 — *Spirit of Man* — Demonstrating the attitude of bitterness.
3:24 — *Spirit* — The Holy Spirit (speaks).
8:3 — *Spirit* — God's spirit demonstrating communications.
10:17 — *Spirit* — A spirit being (future prophecy)
11:1 — *Spirit* — God's spirit demonstrating communications.
11:5 — *Spirit* of the Lord — The Holy Spirit (speaks).
11:19 — *Spirit* — God's spirit (attitude).
11:24 — *Spirit* — A spirit being.
11:24 — *Spirit of God* — Demonstrating communications through a dream.
13:3 — *Spirit of Man* — Demonstrating lack of power and selfish attitude.
18:31 — *Spirit* — A change of attitude.
21:7 — *Spirit* — A mental state of mind.
36:26 — *Spirit* — Spirit of God — a new nature (attitude).
36:27 — *Spirit* — Could represent the Holy Spirit or God's nature.
37:1 — *Spirit* of the Lord — The Holy Spirit.
37:14 — *Spirit* — Spirit of God — a new nature (attitude).
39:29 — *Spirit* — God's spirit or nature.
43:5 — *Spirit* — God's spirit (communications).

DANIEL
2:1 — *Spirit* — Mental state of mind (troubled).
2:3 — *Spirit* — Mental state of mind (troubled).
4:8 — *Spirit* — The Holy Spirit.
4:9 — *Spirit* — The Holy Spirit.
4:18 — *Spirit* — The Holy Spirit.
5:11 — *Spirit* — The Holy Spirit.
5:12 — *Spirit* — Mental state of mind (keen mind or excellent mind).
5:14 — *Spirit* — Representation of God in Daniel.

DANIEL
6:3 — *Spirit* — Mental state of mind (keen mind or excellent mind).
7:15 — *Spirit of Man* — Mental state of mind (troubled).

HOSEA
4:12 — *Spirit of Attitude* — Attitude of prostitution or Idolatry.
5:4 — *Spirit of Attitude* — Attitude of prostitution or Idolatry.

JOEL
2:28 — *Spirit* — Spirit of God (power to see and understand).
2:29 — *Spirit* — Spirit of God (power to see and understand).

MICAH
2:7 — *Spirit of the Lord* — Holy Spirit (referenced as He).
2:11 — *Spirit of Attitude* — An attitude of lying or falsehood.
3:8 — *Spirit of the Lord* — The Holy Spirit providing power.

HAGGAI
1:14 — *Spirit of Man* — Motivated to action.
2:5 — *Spirit* — The Holy Spirit.

ZECHARIAH
4:6 — *Spirit* — Spirit of God (God's nature is the foundation).
6:5 — *Spirit* — Spirit beings (angels).
6:8 — *Spirit* — State of mind (calmed).
7:12 — *Spirit* — God's spirit passed on through the prophets.
12:1 — *Spirit of Man* — Referencing man's life as a whole.
12:10 — *Spirit of Attitude* — The attitude of grace.
13:2 — *Spirit of Attitude* — The attitude of impurity or idolatry.

MALACHI
2:15 — *Spirit* — The nature of man.
2:15 — *Spirit* — Spirit of man in reference to attitude.
2:16 — *Spirit* — Spirit of man in reference to attitude.

APPENDIX B

WORD USAGE OF SPIRIT IN THE NEW TESTAMENT

(Listing the Word "SPIRIT" As Referenced in the King James Bible)

NT: PNEUMA

Appendix Key:

Scripture references are in **BOLD** font type.
Word Categories are in *ITALICS* font type.
Word usage descriptions are in NORMAL font type.

Reference — *Category* — Usage

MATTHEW

3:16 — *Spirit of God* — The Father's spirit in presence and blessing.
4:1 — *Spirit* — The — Father's spirit leading Jesus (communications).
5:3 — *Spirit* — Attitude of humbleness.
10:20 — *Spirit* — God's attitudes being displayed in your speech.
12:18 — *Spirit* — God's spirit bringing authority and power.
12:28 — *Spirit of God* — Displaying the attribute of power.
12:43 — *Unclean Spirit* — Same as evil spirits or demons.
22:43 — *Spirit* — God's nature or presence in King David.
26:41 — *Spirit* — Man's spirit contrasted to man's body.

MARK

1:10 — *Spirit* — The Father's spirit in presence and blessing.
1:12 — *Spirit* — The Father's spirit leading Jesus (communications).
1:23 — *Unclean Spirit* — Same as evil spirits or demons.
1:26 — *Unclean Spirit* — Same as evil spirits or demons.
2:8 — *Spirit* — Jesus' spirit demonstrating omnipresence
3:30 — *Unclean Spirit* — Same as evil spirits or demons.

MARK

5:2 — *UNCLEAN SPIRIT* — SAME AS EVIL SPIRITS OR DEMONS.
5:8 — *Unclean Spirit* — Same as evil spirits or demons.
7:25 — *Spirit* — A spirit being or the spirit world.
8:12 — *Spirit* — Jesus' spirit (attitude of disappointment).
9:17 — *Spirit* — A spirit that took away the individual's speech.
9:20 — *Spirit* — An evil spirit possessing an individual.
9:25 — *Spirit* — An evil spirit possessing an individual.
9:25 — *Spirit* — An evil spirit possessing an individual.
9:26 — *Spirit* — An evil spirit possessing an individual.
14:38 — *Spirit* — Man's spirit contrasted to man's body.

LUKE

1:17 — *Spirit* — God's spirit demonstrating authority and power.
1:47 — *Spirit* — God's spirit in Mary reflecting a worship attitude.
1:80 — *Spirit* — God's spirit in John the Baptist providing strength.
2:27 — *Spirit* — God's spirit leading Jesus (communications).
2:40 — *Spirit* — God's spirit in Jesus providing strength.
4:1 — *Spirit* — God's spirit leading (communications).
4:14 — *Spirit* — God's spirit providing power.
4:18 — *Spirit of the Lord* — The Holy Spirit administering his anointing.
4:33 — *Spirit* — An unclean or evil spirit.
8:29 — *Spirit* — An unclean or evil spirit.
8:55 — *Spirit* — Life.
9:39 — *Spirit* — A demon.
9:42 — *Spirit* — An unclean spirit of demon.
9:55 — *Spirit* — What spirit is your attitude coming from?
10:21 — *Spirit* — Jesus' spirit reflecting and attitude of rejoicing.
11:13 — *Holy Spirit* — The Holy Spirit as a gift.
11:24 — *Spirit* — Unclean or evil spirit.
13:11 — *Spirit* — A spirit being that brings affliction.
23:46 — *Spirit* — Jesus' life on earth.
24:37 — *Spirit* — A spirit being.
24:39 — *Spirit* — A spirit being.

John

1:32 — *Spirit* — God's spirit demonstrating authority and power.
1:33 — *Spirit* — God's spirit demonstrating authority and power.
3:5 — *Spirit* — Born of God's spirit (adoption, new nature)
3:6 — *Spirit* — Spirit nature.
3:6 — *Spirit* — Spirit nature.
3:8 — *Spirit* — God's spirit nature.
3:34 — *Spirit* — Spirit of God providing power.
4:23 — *Spirit* — Spirit of God providing power.
4:24 — *Spirit* — God's spirit nature.
4:24 — *Spirit* — God's spirit nature.
6:63 — *Spirit* — God's nature which is life.
7:39 — *Spirit* — The Holy Spirit.
11:33 — *Spirit* — Jesus spirit demonstrating an attitude of sadness.
13:21 — *Spirit* — Jesus spirit demonstrating an attitude of sadness.
14:17 — *Spirit of truth* — The Holy Spirit.
15:26 — *Spirit of truth* — The Holy Spirit.
16:13 — *Spirit of truth* — The Holy Spirit.

Acts

2:4 — *Spirit* — The Holy Spirit.
2:17 — *Spirit* — God's spirit providing ability.
2:18 — *Spirit* — God's spirit providing ability.
5:9 — *Spirit* of the Lord — The Holy Spirit.
6:10 — *Spirit* — God's spirit demonstrating wisdom (attitude).
7:59 — *Spirit* — Spiritual life.
8:29 — *Spirit* — Holy Spirit spoke to Philip.
8:39 — *Spirit of the Lord* — The Holy Spirit.
10:19 — *Spirit* — The Holy — Spirit spoke to Peter.
11:12 — *Spirit* — The Holy Spirit gave direction.
11:28 — *Spirit* — Spirit of God providing communications.
16:7 — *Spirit* — The Holy Spirit gave direction.
16:16 — *Spirit* — Unclean spirit or demon.
16:18 — *Spirit* — Demon.
17:16 — *Spirit* — He was motivated through his new nature.
18:5 — *Spirit* — He was motivated through his new nature.

ACTS

18:25 — *Spirit* — He was motivated through his new nature.
19:15 — *Evil Spirit* — Demon.
19:16 — *Evil Spirit* — Demon.
19:21 — *Spirit* — He was motivated through his new nature.
20:22 — *Spirit* — He was motivated through his new nature.
21:4 — *Spirit* — Communications through God's nature (authority).
23:8 — *Spirit* — Spirit world of mankind.
23:9 — *Spirit* — Spirit world of God's Kingdom.

ROMANS

1:4 — *Spirit of Holiness* — Same as spirit of God or God's nature which is holy.
1:9 — *Spirit* — Serve with my spirit or attitude.
2:29 — *Spirit* — Spirit of attitude in contrast to the letter of the law.
7:6 — *Spirit* — Spirit of a new attitude that comes from God.
8:1 — *Spirit* — New nature vs. the old nature represented by flesh.
8:2 — *Spirit* — Representing eternal life.
8:4 — *Spirit* — New nature vs. the old nature represented by flesh.
8:5 — *Spirit* — God's nature.
8:5 — *Spirit* — God's nature.
8:9 — *Spirit* — God's nature.
8:9 — *Spirit of God* — God's nature (the same as the spirit of Christ).
8:9 — *Spirit of Christ* — God's nature (the same as the spirit of God).
8:10 — *Spirit* — Representing eternal life vs. physical death.
8:11 — *Spirit* — God's nature.
8:11 — *Spirit* — God's nature demonstrating power.
8:13 — *Spirit* — God's nature or new nature vs. old nature or flesh.
8:14 — *Spirit of God* — God's nature.
8:15 — *Spirit* — Old nature or spirit of man.
8:15 — *Spirit* — New nature or spirit of God.
8:16 — *Spirit* — The Holy Spirit.
8:16 — *Spirit* — Representing self (a mental state of communications).
8:23 — *Spirit* — God's nature.
8:26 — *Spirit* — The Holy Spirit helping.
8:26 — *Spirit* — The Holy Spirit making intercession.

ROMANS

8:27 — *Spirit* — The Holy Spirit.
11:8 — *Spirit* — An attitude of slumber or lack of wisdom to see.
12:11 — *Spirit* — A fervent attitude.
15:19 — *Spirit of God* — Demonstrating power.
15:30 — *Spirit* — God's nature that brings holiness and power.

I CORINTHIANS

2:4 — *Spirit* — Representing God's nature brings wisdom and power.
2:10 — *Spirit* — God's nature.
2:10 — *Spirit* — God's nature.
2:11 — *Spirit of Man* — Man's nature providing motives man can only know.
2:11 — *Spirit of God* — God's nature referencing back to verse 10.
2:12 — *Spirit* — Old nature.
2:12 — *Spirit* — New nature.
2:14 — *Spirit of God* — God's nature.
3:16 — *Spirit of God* — God's nature.
4:21 — *Spirit* — The attitude of meekness.
5:3 — *Spirit* — To be one in attitude and mind set.
5:4 — *Spirit* — To be one in attitude and mind set.
5:5 — *Spirit* — Representing life in an eternal state.
6:11 — *Spirit* — God's nature.
6:17 — *Spirit* — One in mind or one in nature (bring unity).
6:20 — *Spirit* — Representing spiritual life.
7:34 — *Spirit* — Representing spiritual unity in attitudes or motives.
7:40 — *Spirit of God* — God's nature.
12:3 — *Spirit of God* — God's nature will not allow you to deny Jesus as God.
12:4 — *Spirit* — God's nature bringing unity.
12:7 — *Spirit* — The Holy Spirit who brings us God's nature.
12:8 — *Spirit* — The Holy Spirit who brings us God's nature.
12:8 — *Spirit* — The Holy Spirit who brings us God's nature.
12:9 — *Spirit* — The Holy Spirit who brings us God's nature.
12:9 — *Spirit* — The Holy Spirit who brings us God's nature.
12:11 — *Spirit* — The Holy Spirit.

I Corinthians

12:13 — *Spirit* — The Holy Spirit who brings us God's nature.
12:13 — *Spirit* — The Holy Spirit who brings us God's nature.
14:2 — *Spirit* — Man's spirit used to communicate with God's spirit.
14:14 — *Spirit* — Providing motivation.
14:15 — *Spirit* — Providing motivation.
14:15 — *Spirit* — Providing motivation.
14:16 — *Spirit* — Providing motivation.
15:45 — *Spirit* — Jesus the giver of eternal life vs. Adam's physical life.
16:18 — *Spirit* — Representing a spirit of attitude or new motivation.

II Corinthians

1:22 — *Spirit* — The Holy Spirit (representing a seal).
2:13 — *Spirit* — A state of mind or calmness of mind.
3:3 — *Spirit* — God's nature demonstrated in Paul's life or ministry.
3:6 — *Spirit* — God's spirit or nature.
3:6 — *Spirit* — God's nature.
3:8 — *Spirit* — The Holy Spirit's ministry.
3:17 — *Spirit* — The Holy Spirit.
3:17 — *Spirit of the Lord* — The Holy Spirit.
3:18 — *Spirit of the Lord* — The Holy Spirit allowing us to show God's image.
4:13 — *Spirit* — Reflective of God's nature.
5:5 — *Spirit* — The Holy Spirit.
7:1 — *Spirit* — Representing spiritual life.
7:13 — *Spirit* — Refreshed or newly motivated.
11:4 — *Spirit* — Representing a different attitude.
12:18 — *Spirit* — Representing attitude.

Galatians

3:2 — *Spirit* — The Holy Spirit.
3:3 — *Spirit* — The Holy Spirit.
3:5 — *Spirit* — The Holy Spirit.
3:14 — *Spirit* — The Holy Spirit.
4:6 — *Spirit* — God's nature same as spirit of Christ.
4:29 — *Spirit* — God's nature.

GALATIANS

5:5 — *Spirit* — The work of the Holy Spirit.
5:16 — *Spirit* — God's nature.
5:17 — *Spirit* — Two natures warring against each other.
5:17 — *Spirit* — Two natures warring against each other.
5:18 — *Spirit* — Lead by the Holy Spirit.
5:22 — *Spirit* — Holy Spirit the provider of God's nature.
5:25 — *Spirit* — God's nature.
5:25 — *Spirit* — God's nature.
6:1 — *Spirit* — Spirit of attitude of meekness.
6:8 — *Spirit* — God's nature.
6:8 — *Spirit* — God's nature.
6:18 — *Spirit* — Representing man's spiritual life.

EPHESIANS

1:13 — *holy Spirit* — The Holy Spirit.
1:17 — *Spirit of Wisdom* — God's spirit brings wisdom for understanding.
2:2 — *Spirit* — Satan working on man's spirit to sin (attitude).
2:18 — *Spirit* — God's spirit or nature in us is bringing unity.
2:22 — *Spirit* — God's nature comes to us through Christ.
3:5 — *Spirit* — The Holy Spirit teaching us.
3:16 — *Spirit* — God's nature in us brought by the Holy Spirit.
4:3 — *Spirit* — Unity of Attitude.
4:4 — *Spirit* — Representing the whole person, promoting unity.
4:23 — *Spirit* — Attitude stemming through the new nature.
4:30 — *holy Spirit* — The person of the Holy Spirit.
5:9 — *Spirit* — God's nature produces these attitudes of attributes.
5:18 — *Spirit* — God's nature providing proper attitude for worship.
6:17 — *Spirit* — Holy Spirit who uses the word of God for conviction.
6:18 — *Spirit* — Through your new nature and the Holy Spirit.

PHILIPPIANS

1:19 — *Spirit of Christ* — God's nature as found in Jesus Christ.
1:27 — *Spirit* — Spirit of unity or attitude produced by God's nature.
2:1 — *Spirit* — Worship God through his nature in believers.
3:3 — *Spirit* — Worship God through his nature in believers.

COLOSSIANS
1:8 — *Spirit* — Love stemming from God's nature in believers.
2:5 — *Spirit* — Spirit of unity, stemming from God's nature in them.

I THESSALONIANS
5:19 — *Spirit* — God's nature in believers providing proper motives.
5:23 — *Spirit* — Spirit of attitude produced by God's nature in us.

II THESSALONIANS
2:2 — *Spirit* — Spirit of attitude (do not be influenced by attitudes).
2:8 — *Spirit* — By the power of God's very nature.
2:12 — *Spirit* — Holy Spirit, whose work is to sanctify the believer.

I TIMOTHY
3:16 — *Spirit* — God's nature which is just and holy.
4:1 — *Spirit* — The Holy Spirit speaks.
4:12 — *Spirit* — Spirit of attitude stemming from God's nature.

II TIMOTHY
1:7 — *Spirit* — Spirit of attitude stemming from God's nature.
4:22 — *Spirit* — May Christ protect your spirit of attitude.

PHILEMON
v25 — *Spirit* — May Christ protect your spirit of attitude.

HEBREWS
4:12 — *Spirit* — Spirit of man. That part of us that provide motives.
9:14 — *Spirit* — God's eternal nature represented in Christ.
10:29 — *Spirit* — God's attitude of grace produced by his nature.

JAMES
2:26 — *Spirit* — Spirit of life or man's spiritual nature.
4:5 — *Spirit* — The Holy Spirit who lives in believers.

I PETER
1:2 — *Spirit* — Man's new nature separated from the old nature.

I PETER

1:11 — *Spirit of Christ* — God's nature in believers.
1:22 — *Spirit* — Through God's nature providing proper motives.
3:4 — *Spirit* — Attitude produced by one's new nature.
3:18 — *Spirit* — Holy Spirit who brings life and convicts of sin.
4:6 — *Spirit* — In regard to God's nature producing good attributes.
4:14 — *Spirit of Glory* — God's nature and all the glory it.

I JOHN

3:24 — *Spirit* — The Holy Spirit that indwells believers.
4:1 — *Spirit* — Spirit of attitude that can only be from God's nature.
4:2 — *Spirit of God* — Know God's nature and the attitudes it produces.
4:2 — *Spirit* — Any attitude recognizing Christ is God is from God.
4:3 — *Spirit* — Any attitude rejecting Christ as God is not from God.
4:3 — *Spirit* — This attitude is from Satan or those that follow him.
4:6 — *Spirit* — An attitude representing God's truth.
4:6 — *Spirit* — An attitude not representing God's truth.
4:13 — *Spirit* — God's nature providing God's attitudes (love).
5:6 — *Spirit* — The Holy Spirit testifies to the world of God's truth.
5:6 — *Spirit* of Truth — God's nature is the foundation of truth.
5:8 — *Spirit* — Holy Spirit testifies to the world who Jesus is.

JUDE

v19 — *Spirit* — God's nature brought by the Holy Spirit.

REVELATION

1:10 — *Spirit* — State of mind with God communicating his will.
2:7 — *Spirit* — Sent angel to speak. (Rev. 22:17)
2:11 — *Spirit* — Sent angel to speak. (Rev. 22:17)
2:29 — *Spirit* — Sent angel to speak. (Rev. 22:17)
3:6 — *Spirit* — Sent angel to speak. (Rev. 22:17)
3:13 — *Spirit* — Sent angel to speak. (Rev. 22:17)
3:13 — *Spirit* — Sent angel to speak. (Rev. 22:17) will.
4:2 — *Spirit* — State of mind with God communicating his
11:11 — *Spirit* — God restoring physical life to their bodies.
14:13 — *Spirit* — The Holy Spirit speaks.

Revelation

17:3 — *Spirit* — State of mind with God communicating his will.
18:2 — *Spirit* — Evil attitudes representing Satan and his mind set.
19:10 — *Spirit* — Attitude behind the prophecy.
21:10 — *Spirit* — State of mind with God communicating his will.
22:17 — *Spirit* — An angel.

APPENDIX C

WORD USAGE OF SOUL IN THE OLD TESTAMENT

(Listing the Word "SOUL" As Referenced in the King James Bible)

OT: NEPHESH

Appendix Key:

Scripture references are in **BOLD** font type.
Word usage descriptions are in NORMAL font type.

Reference — Usage

GENESIS
2:7 — Representing personhood.
12:13 — Representing personhood.
17:14 — Representing personhood.
19:20 — Representing personhood.
27:4 — Representing personhood.
27:19 — Representing personhood.
27:25 — Representing personhood.
27:31 — Representing personhood.
34:3 — Representing personhood.
35:18 — Representing a person that is dying.
42:21 — Soul demonstrating emotion.
49:6 — Representing personhood.

EXODUS
12:15 — Representing personhood.
12:19 — Representing personhood.
30:12 — Representing the spiritual life of person. That part that lives after death.

EXODUS
31:14 — Representing personhood.

LEVITICUS
4:2 — Representing personhood.
5:1 — Representing personhood.
5:2 — Representing personhood.
5:4 — Representing personhood.
5:12 — Representing personhood.
5:17 — Representing personhood.
6:2 — Representing personhood.
7:18 — Representing personhood.
7:20 — Representing personhood.
7:20 — Representing personhood.
7:21 — Representing personhood.
7:25 — Representing personhood.
7:27 — Representing personhood.
7:27 — Representing personhood.
17:10 — Representing personhood.
17:11 — Representing personhood.
17:12 — Representing personhood.
17:15 — Representing personhood.
19:8 — Representing personhood.
20:6 — Representing personhood.
20:6 — Representing personhood.
22:3 — Representing personhood.
22:6 — Representing personhood.
22:11 — Representing personhood.
23:29 — Representing personhood.
23:30 — Representing personhood.
23:30 — Representing personhood.
26:11 — Representing God the Father's soul or personhood.
26:15 — Representing personhood.
26:30 — Representing God the Father's soul or personhood.
26:43 — Representing personhood.

NUMBERS
9:13 — Representing personhood.
11:6 — Representing personhood.
15:27 — Representing personhood.
15:28 — Representing personhood.
15:30 — Representing personhood.
15:30 — Representing personhood.
15:31 — Representing personhood.
19:13 — Representing personhood.
19:20 — Representing personhood.
19:22 — Representing personhood.
21:4 — Representing personhood.
21:5 — Representing personhood.
30:2 — Representing personhood.
30:4 — Representing personhood.
30:5 — Representing personhood.
30:6 — Representing personhood.
30:7 — Representing personhood.
30:8 — Representing personhood.
30:10 — Representing personhood.
30:11 — Representing personhood.
30:12 — Representing personhood.
30:13 — Representing personhood.
31:28 — Representing personhood.

DEUTERONOMY
4:9 — Representing personhood.
4:29 — Representing personhood.
6:5 — Representing personhood.
10:12 — Representing personhood.
11:13 — Representing personhood.
11:18 — Representing personhood.
12:15 — Representing personhood.
12:20 — Representing personhood.
12:20 — Soul demonstrating lust, a product of mankind's personhood.
12:21 — Soul demonstrating lust, a product of mankind's personhood.

DEUTERONOMY
13:3 — Representing personhood.
13:6 — Representing personhood.
14:26 — Soul demonstrating lust, a product of mankind's personhood.
14:26 — Representing personhood.
26:16 — Representing personhood.
30:2 — Representing personhood.
30:6 — Representing personhood.
30:10 — Representing personhood.

JOSHUA
22:5 — Representing personhood.

JUDGES
5:21 — Representing personhood.
10:16 — Representing God the Father's soul grieving.
16:16 — Representing personhood.

I SAMUEL
1:10 — Representing personhood.
1:15 — Representing personhood.
1:26 — Representing personhood.
2:16 — Representing personhood.
17:55 — Representing personhood.
18:1 — Representing personhood.
18:1 — Representing personhood.
18:1 — Representing personhood.
18:3 — Representing personhood.
20:3 — Representing personhood.
20:4 — Representing personhood.
20:17 — Representing personhood.
23:20 — Representing personhood.
24:11 — Representing personhood.
25:26 — Representing personhood.
25:29 — Representing personhood.
26:21 — Representing personhood.
30:6 — Representing personhood.

II Samuel
4:9 — Representing personhood.
5:8 — Representing personhood.
11:11 — Representing personhood.
13:39 — Representing personhood.
14:19 — Representing personhood.

I Kings
1:29 — Soul demonstrating emotion (distress).
2:4 — Representing personhood.
8:48 — Representing personhood.
11:37 — Soul demonstrating desire. A product of personhood.
17:21 — Representing personhood.
17:22 — Representing personhood.

II Kings
2:2 — Representing personhood.
2:4 — Representing personhood.
2:6 — Representing personhood.
4:27 — Representing personhood.
4:30 — Representing personhood.
23:3 — Representing personhood.
23:5 — Representing personhood.

I Chronicles
22:19 — Soul demonstrating the act of the will.

II Chronicles
6:38 — Representing personhood.
15:12 — Representing personhood.
34:31 — Representing personhood.

Job
3:20 — Representing personhood.
6:7 — Soul demonstrating the act of the will.
7:11 — Representing personhood.
7:15 — Soul demonstrating the act of the will.

Job

9:21 — Representing personhood.
10:1 — Representing personhood.
10:1 — Representing personhood.
12:10 — Representing personhood.
14:22 — Representing personhood.
16:4 — Representing personhood.
19:2 — Representing personhood.
21:25 — Representing personhood.
23:13 — Representing personhood.
24:12 — Representing personhood.
27:2 — Representing personhood.
27:8 — Representing personhood.
30:15 — Representing personhood.
30:16 — Representing personhood.
30:25 — Soul showing emotion (grieve).
31:30 — Representing personhood.
33:18 — Representing personhood.
33:28 — Representing personhood.
33:30 — Representing personhood.

Psalms

3:2 — Representing personhood.
6:3 — Representing personhood.
6:4 — Representing personhood.
7:2 — Representing personhood.
7:5 — Representing personhood.
11:1 — Representing personhood.
11:5 — Representing God the Father's soul or personhood.
13:2 — Soul demonstrating intellect or reasoning ability.
16:2 — Representing personhood.
16:10 — Representing personhood.
17:13 — Representing personhood.
19:7 — Representing personhood.
22:20 — Representing personhood.
22:29 — Representing personhood.
23:3 — Representing personhood.

Psalms

24:4 — Representing personhood.
25:1 — Representing personhood.
25:13 — Representing personhood.
25:20 — Representing personhood.
26:9 — Representing personhood.
30:3 — Representing personhood.
31:7 — Representing personhood.
31:9 — Soul demonstrating emotion.
33:19 — Representing personhood.
33:20 — Representing personhood.
34:2 — Representing personhood.
34:22 — Representing personhood.
35:3 — Representing personhood.
35:4 — Representing personhood.
35:7 — Representing personhood.
35:9 — Soul demonstrating the emotion of rejoicing.
35:12 — Soul demonstrating emotion (forlorn — sad or lonely).
35:13 — Representing personhood.
35:17 — Representing personhood.
40:14 — Representing personhood.
41:4 — Representing personhood.
42:1 — Representing personhood.
42:2 — Representing personhood.
42:4 — Representing personhood.
42:5 — Representing personhood.
42:6 — Representing personhood.
42:11 — Representing personhood.
43:5 — Representing personhood.
44:25 — Representing personhood.
49:15 — Representing personhood.
49:18 — Representing personhood.
54:3 — Representing personhood.
54:4 — Representing personhood.
55:18 — Representing personhood.
56:6 — Representing personhood.
56:13 — Representing personhood.

PSALMS

57:1 — Representing personhood.
57:4 — Representing personhood.
57:6 — Representing personhood.
59:3 — Representing personhood.
62:1 — Representing personhood.
62:5 — Representing personhood.
63:1 — Representing personhood.
63:5 — Representing personhood.
63:8 — Representing personhood.
63:9 — Representing personhood.
66:9 — Representing personhood.
66:16 — Representing personhood.
69:1 — Representing personhood.
69:10 — Representing personhood.
69:18 — Representing personhood.
70:2 — Representing personhood.
71:10 — Representing personhood.
71:13 — Representing personhood.
71:23 — Representing personhood.
72:14 — Representing personhood.
74:19 — Representing personhood.
77:2 — Representing personhood.
78:50 — Representing personhood.
84:2 — Representing personhood.
86:2 — Representing personhood.
86:4 — Representing personhood.
86:13 — Representing personhood.
86:14 — Representing personhood.
88:3 — Representing personhood.
88:14 — Representing personhood.
89:48 — Representing personhood.
94:17 — Representing personhood.
94:19 — Representing personhood.
94:21 — Representing personhood.
103:1 — Representing personhood.
103:2 — Representing personhood.

Psalms

103:22 — Representing personhood.
104:1 — Representing personhood.
104:35 — Representing personhood.
106:15 — Representing personhood.
107:5 — Representing personhood.
107:9 — Representing personhood.
107:9 — Representing personhood.
107:18 — Representing personhood.
107:26 — Representing personhood.
109:20 — Representing personhood.
116:4 — Representing personhood.
116:7 — Representing personhood.
116:8 — Representing personhood.
119:20 — Representing personhood.
119:25 — Representing personhood.
119:28 — Representing personhood.
119:81 — Representing personhood.
119:109 — Representing personhood.
119:129 — Representing personhood.
119:167 — Representing personhood.
119:175 — Representing personhood.
102:2 — Representing personhood.
102:6 — Representing personhood.
121:7 — Representing personhood.
123:4 — Representing personhood.
124:4 — Representing personhood.
124:5 — Representing personhood.
124:7 — Representing personhood.
130:5 — Representing personhood.
130:6 — Representing personhood.
131:2 — Representing personhood.
138:3 — Representing personhood.
139:14 — Soul demonstrating intellect (knowledge)
141:8 — Representing personhood.
142:4 — Representing personhood.
142:7 — Representing personhood.

PSALMS
143:3 — Representing personhood.
143:6 — Representing personhood.
143:8 — Representing personhood.
143:11 — Representing personhood.
143:12 — Representing personhood.
146:1 — Soul demonstrating intellect, emotion and will (demonstrated by worship).

PROVERBS
2:10 — Soul demonstrating intellectual ability through holding knowledge.
3:22 — Representing personhood.
6:30 — Representing personhood.
6:32 — Representing personhood.
8:36 — Representing personhood.
10:3 — Representing personhood.
11:17 — Representing personhood.
11:25 — Representing personhood.
13:2 — Representing personhood.
13:4 — Representing personhood.
13:4 — Representing personhood.
13:19 — Representing personhood.
13:25 — Representing personhood.
15:32 — Representing personhood.
16:17 — Representing personhood.
16:24 — Soul and body being differentiated.
18:7 — Representing personhood.
19:2 — Soul in reference to having knowledge — Intellect.
19:8 — Representing personhood.
19:15 — Representing personhood.
19:16 — Representing personhood.
19:18 — Representing personhood.
20:2 — Representing personhood.
21:10 — Soul demonstrating will (desire).
21:23 — Representing personhood.
22:5 — Representing personhood.

Proverbs

22:23 — Representing personhood.
22:25 — Representing personhood.
23:14 — Representing personhood.
24:12 — Representing personhood.
24:14 — Soul demonstrating intellect (reasoning).
25:13 — Representing personhood.
25:25 — Representing personhood.
27:7 — Representing personhood.
27:7 — Representing personhood experiencing hunger.
29:10 — Representing personhood.
29:17 — Soul displaying emotion (delight).
29:24 — Representing personhood.

Ecclesiastes

2:24 — Soul demonstrating emotion (enjoying, being happy).
4:8 — Representing personhood.
6:2 — Representing personhood.
6:3 — Representing personhood.
7:28 — Soul displaying an act of the will (it seeketh).

Song of Solomon

1.7 — Soul demonstrating the emotional side of love.
3.1 — Soul demonstrating the emotional side of love.
3.2 — Soul demonstrating the emotional side of love.
3.3 — Soul demonstrating the emotional side of love.
3.4 — Soul demonstrating the emotional side of love.
5.6 — Representing personhood.
6.12 — Representing personhood.

Isaiah

1.14 — Soul representing the whole person in the act of hate.
3.9 — Representing personhood.
10.18 — A distinction between soul and body.
26.8 — Representing personhood.
26.9 — Representing personhood.
29.8 — Representing personhood.

Isaiah

29.8 — Representing personhood.
32.6 — Representing personhood.
38.15 — Soul representing the whole person in the act of being bitter.
38.17 — Representing personhood.
42.1 — Soul demonstrating the emotion of delight.
44.2 — Representing personhood.
51.23 — Representing personhood.
53.10 — Representing personhood.
53.11 — Representing personhood.
53.12 — Representing personhood.
55.2 — Soul demonstrating the emotion of delight.
55.3 — Representing personhood.
58.3 — Representing personhood.
58.5 — Representing personhood.
58.10 — Representing personhood.
58.10 — Representing personhood.
58.11 — Representing personhood.
61.10 — Soul representing the whole person in the act of joy.
66.3 — Soul demonstrating the emotion of delight.

Jeremiah

4:10 — Representing personhood.
4:19 — Representing personhood.
4:31 — Representing personhood.
5:9 — Referencing God the Fathers soul.
5:29 — Referencing God the Father's soul.
6:8 — Referencing God the Father's soul.
9:9 — Referencing God the Father's soul.
12:7 — Representing personhood.
13:17 — Soul demonstrating emotion (weeping).
14:19 — Soul demonstrating the emotion of loathing.
18:20 — Representing personhood.
20:13 — Representing personhood.
31:12 — Representing personhood.
31:14 — Representing personhood.
31:25 — Representing personhood.

JEREMIAH
31:25 — Soul demonstrating the emotion of sorrow.
32:41 — Representing personhood.
38:16 — Soul representing life itself.
38:17 — Representing personhood.
38:20 — Representing personhood.
50:19 — Representing personhood.
51:6 — Representing personhood.
51:45 — Representing personhood.

LAMENTATIONS
1:11 — Representing personhood.
1:16 — Representing personhood.
2:12 — Representing personhood.
3:17 — Representing personhood.
3:20 — Soul in reference to having memory — intellect tied to reasoning of memory.
3:24 — Representing personhood.
3:25 — Representing personhood.
3:58 — Representing personhood.

EZEKIEL
3:19 — Representing personhood.
3:21 — Representing personhood.
4:14 — Representing personhood.
18:4 — Representing personhood.
18:4 — Representing personhood.
18:4 — Representing personhood.
18:20 — Representing personhood.
18:27 — Representing personhood.
24:21 — Representing personhood.
33:5 — Representing personhood.
33:9 — Representing personhood.

HOSEA
9:4 — Representing personhood.

Jonah
2:5 — Representing personhood.

Micah
2:7 — Representing personhood.
6:7 — Soul and body being differentiated.
7:1 — Soul demonstrating the act of the will.

Habakkuk
2:4 — Representing personhood.
2:10 — Representing personhood.

Zechariah
11:8 — Representing personhood.
11:8 — Representing personhood.

APPENDIX D

LISTING WORD USAGE OF SOUL IN THE NEW TESTAMENT

(Listing the Word "SOUL" As Referenced in the King James Bible)

NT: PSUCHE

Appendix Key:

Scripture reference books are in **BOLD** font type.
Word usage descriptions are in NORMAL font type.

Reference — Usage

MATTHEW
10:28 — Representing life after death. Soul is separate from the body.
10:28 — Representing life after death. Soul is separate from the body.
12:18 — O.T. quote of God the Father's soul showing emotion (He is pleased).
16:26 — Soul representing personhood.
16:26 — Soul representing personhood.
22:37 — Soul representing personhood separate from heart and mind.
26:38 — Jesus' soul demonstrating emotion.

MARK
8:36 — Soul representing personhood.
8:37 — Soul representing personhood.
12:30 — Soul representing personhood.
12:33 — Soul representing personhood.
14:34 — Jesus' soul demonstrating emotion.

LUKE
1:46 — Soul demonstrating worship an act of the will.

LUKE
2:35 — Soul demonstrating personhood.
10:27 — Soul demonstrating love to be applied through intellect, emotion and will.
12:19 — Soul holding conversation demonstrating intellect.
12:19 — Soul holding conversation demonstrating intellect.
12:20 — Soul representing personhood.

JOHN
12:27 — Jesus' soul demonstrating emotion.

ACTS
2:27 — Jesus' soul as spoken of in prophecy.
2:31 — Jesus' soul as spoken of by the Apostle Peter.
2:43 — Soul representing personhood.
3:23 — Soul representing personhood.
4:32 — Soul demonstrating that belief is an act of the will.

ROMANS
2:9 — Soul representing personhood.
13:1 — Soul representing personhood.

I CORINTHIANS
15:45 — Soul representing personhood.

II CORINTHIANS
1:23 — Soul representing personhood.

I THESSALONIANS
5:23 — Soul representing personhood (soul as different from spirit and body).

HEBREWS
4:12 — Soul as in different from spirit and represents that part producing thought.
6:19 — Soul representing personhood.

Hebrews
10:38 — O.T. quote speaking of God the Father's soul demonstrating emotion.
10:39 — Soul representing personhood (speaking to the saving of the soul).

James
5:20 — Soul representing personhood.

I Peter
2:1 — Soul representing personhood.

II Peter
2:8 — Soul showing emotion (being vexed).

III John
1:2 — Soul representing personhood.

Revelation
16:3 — Soul representing personhood.
18:14 — Soul representing personhood. (Demonstrating that lust is a product of intellect, emotion, and will.)

SCRIPTURE INDEX

All Scriptures indexed are in alphanumeric order and reference the New American Standard Bible (NASB) of 1960 unless otherwise noted.

" * " Indicates the passage is quoted on that page for discussion.

1

1 Corinthians 10:14-17 35
1 Corinthians 10:20-22 * 125
1 Corinthians 12 124
1 Corinthians 12:9 169
1 Corinthians 13:4-7 * 58
1 Corinthians 13:9-10 * 113
1 Corinthians 15:13-14 101
1 Corinthians 15:1-8 154
1 Corinthians 15:35-39 100
1 Corinthians 15:35-39 * 99
1 Corinthians 15:35-44 .... 130, 132
1 Corinthians 15:45-47 171
1 Corinthians 15:45-49 158
1 Corinthians 15:46 .... 142, 146
1 Corinthians 15:49-58 150
1 Corinthians 15:51 27
1 Corinthians 2:10-11 59
1 Corinthians 2:10-16 81
1 Corinthians 2:11 43
1 Corinthians 2:11 * 165
1 Corinthians 2:11-14 * 23
1 Corinthians 2:13 47
1 Corinthians 2:16 59
1 Corinthians 4:21 43
1 Corinthians 4:9-13 169
1 Corinthians 6:16-17 59
1 Corinthians 6:18 105
1 Corinthians 6:18-19 64
1 Corinthians 6:19 .... 28, 39, 77
1 Corinthians 7:1-5 164

1 John 2:16 105
1 John 2:18-23; 4:1-3; 5:20 36
1 John 3:19-20 * 82
1 John 4:14 153
1 John 4:4 * KJV 126
1 John 4:8 57
1 Kings 11:6 122
1 Kings 22:21 38
1 Kings 3:7-12 122
1 Kings 8:30 76
1 Peter 1:23 149
1 Peter 1:3-9 150
1 Peter 1:8-11 * 46
1 Peter 2:24-25 * 174
1 Peter 3:18-22 77
1 Peter 3:22 175
1 Peter 5:10 52
1 Peter 5:1-5 164
1 Peter 5:5 169
1 Peter 5:8 168
1 Samuel 1:15 * KJV 107
1 Samuel 16:14 38
1 Samuel 16:7 115
1 Samuel 2:2 55
1 Thessalonians 5:23 .... 48, 99
1 Thessalonians 5:23 * KJV 63
1 Timothy 1:3-7 166
1 Timothy 3:1-13 164

2

2 Chronicles 12:7 75
2 Chronicles 30:20 75

SCRIPTURE INDEX

2 Corinthians 1:22 28
2 Corinthians 1:24 120
2 Corinthians 10:3-6 124
2 Corinthians 12:2 76
2 Corinthians 12:8-9 169
2 Corinthians 3:17 43
2 Corinthians 3:17 * KJV 43
2 Corinthians 4:18 52
2 Corinthians 4:18 * 53
2 Corinthians 5:16-21 156
2 Corinthians 5:17 .... 121, 149
2 Corinthians 5:17-19 45
2 Corinthians 5:21 .... 86, 107
2 John v7-9 36
2 Kings 2:9 38
2 Kings 22:15-20 50
2 Peter 1:1-4 121
2 Peter 1:2-11 * NIV 176
2 Peter 1:21-22 22
2 Peter 1:4 .... 86, 107
2 Peter 1:4 * 45
2 Samuel 23:2 43
2 Samuel 7:10-17 92
2 Samuel 7:14-17 155
2 Thessalonians 2:1-12 * 28
2 Thessalonians 2:7-10 27
2 Timothy 1:14 123
2 Timothy 1:14 * 77
2 Timothy 1:7 59
2 Timothy 2:13 .... 26, 51, 128, 173
2 Timothy 3:16 .... 22, 35

3

3 John 11 98
3 John 11-12 * 44

A

Acts 1:1-6 77
Acts 1:3 175
Acts 1:6-11 .... 127, 172
Acts 1:8 124
Acts 10:9-16 55
Acts 11:26 36
Acts 13:26-39 155
Acts 15:28 * 74
Acts 16:6 47
Acts 17:2 35
Acts 18:4, 19 35
Acts 2:27 69
Acts 2:31 69
Acts 2:32-36; 7:56 77
Acts 2:33-34 155
Acts 2:33-36, ... 93
Acts 20:18-21 121
Acts 26:28 36
Acts 3:18-26 155
Acts 3:19-26 53
Acts 3:22-26 .... 85, 91
Acts 3:22-26, 10:43 46
Acts 3:25 154
Acts 4:12 121
Acts 8:18-24 168
Acts 8:26 46

C

Colossians 1:13-20 53
Colossians 1:16-17 33
Colossians 1:17 * 33
Colossians 1:18-29 77
Colossians 1:19-22 115
Colossians 1:22 55
Colossians 1:24-27 39
Colossians 1:26-27 27
Colossians 1:27 28
Colossians 1:4 120
Colossians 2:9-11 150
Colossians 3:1 175
Colossians 3:23-24 24

D

Daniel 12:2 100
Daniel 2:1, 3 43

SCRIPTURE INDEX | 223

Daniel 3:20-27 * 172
Daniel 4:34-36 35
Daniel 7:13-14 53
Daniel 9:25-26 172
Deuteronomy 1:9-17 164
Deuteronomy 18:18-20 155
Deuteronomy 18:9-13 126
Deuteronomy 32:17 125
Deuteronomy 33:27 52
Deuteronomy 34:9 38
Deuteronomy 6:4 * 39
Deuteronomy 8:11-14 * 116

E

Ecclesiastes 1:4 53
Ecclesiastes 12:7 .... 38, 144
Ecclesiastes 12:7 * KJV 134
Ephesians 1:13-14 127
Ephesians 1:20 175
Ephesians 1:5 28
Ephesians 2:1-22 149
Ephesians 2:1-9 45
Ephesians 2:1-9 * 108
Ephesians 2:3 56
Ephesians 2:4-7 56
Ephesians 2:8 121
Ephesians 3:1-12 39
Ephesians 3:1-13 27
Ephesians 3:14-19 * 47
Ephesians 3:16 59
Ephesians 4: 11-12 164
Ephesians 4:24 121
Ephesians 4:26 59
Ephesians 4:30 .... 28, 39, 47, 128
Ephesians 4:30 * 75, 86
Ephesians 4:8-10 * 175
Ephesians 5:22 * KJV 90
Ephesians 5:25 90
Ephesians 5:32 27
Ephesians 5:8 118

Ephesians 6:1 * 90
Exodus 10:13 37
Exodus 15:11 55
Exodus 15:8 37
Exodus 2:24 75
Exodus 3:14 KJV 175
Exodus 3:4 75
Exodus 31 and 35 43
Exodus 34:6-7 KJV 56
Exodus 39:1 55
Exodus 4:11 35
Exodus 4:11 * 167
Ezekiel 11:5 43
Ezekiel 13:3 43
Ezekiel 26:20 and 32:24 174
Ezekiel 28:13-17 104
Ezekiel 28:13-17 * 103
Ezekiel 28:17 * 104
Ezekiel 36:22-28 93
Ezra 1:5 * 58
Ezra 5:12 50
Ezra 9:15 55

G

Galatians 3:8-9 91
Galatians 3:8-9 * 154
Galatians 4:8-9 * 119
Galatians 5:16-24 128
Galatians 5:22 127
Galatians 5:22-24 * 58
Genesis 1:1 .... 32, 161
Genesis 1:2 38
Genesis 1:2 * 41
Genesis 1:24-27 * 80
Genesis 1:26 .... 91, 145, 172
Genesis 1:26 * 154
Genesis 1:26 and 27 147
Genesis 1:26-27 143
Genesis 1:26-27 * 141
Genesis 1:27 .... 142, 147

SCRIPTURE INDEX

Genesis 1:3 165
Genesis 1:4, 10, 12, 18, 21, 25, 31 .56
Genesis 12:1-3 91
Genesis 12:1-3 and 17:1-8 154
Genesis 12:3 .... 91, 155
Genesis 16:9 46
Genesis 17:1-8 91
Genesis 2:20 * 113
Genesis 2:24 164
Genesis 2:7 .... 67, 98, 144
Genesis 2:7 KJV 100
Genesis 21:16-20 75
Genesis 3:14-19 .... 53, 98
Genesis 3:15 53
Genesis 3:1-7 104
Genesis 3:1-7 * 103
Genesis 3:17-19 53
Genesis 3:19 53
Genesis 3:22 * 148
Genesis 3:5 105
Genesis 3:5-7 56
Genesis 3:8 37
Genesis 3:8-24 53
Genesis 37:35 174
Genesis 49:18 121
Genesis 6:17 100
Genesis 6:5 75
Genesis 7:21-22 38

H

Habakkuk 1:12 55
Hebrews 1:1-3 33
Hebrews 1:1-4 .... 86, 107
Hebrews 1:3 175
Hebrews 10:12-17 39
Hebrews 10:38 68
Hebrews 11:6 * 119
Hebrews 2:6-10 77
Hebrews 2:6-9 100
Hebrews 2:7-9 156
Hebrews 4:12 * 64

Hebrews 4:15 171
Hebrews 6:13-20 49
Hebrews 6:14-16 51
Hebrews 6:20 and 7:17 155
Hebrews 6:4 124
Hebrews 7:21 49

I

Isaiah 1:18 35
Isaiah 14:9 174
Isaiah 2:11-12 169
Isaiah 2:17 105
Isaiah 26:19 100
Isaiah 26:9 38
Isaiah 29:16 * 162
Isaiah 3:10-11, 32:17 84
Isaiah 42:6 91
Isaiah 42:8 * 43
Isaiah 50:6, 52:13-14, 53 46
Isaiah 53:12 * 174
Isaiah 53:3-6 154
Isaiah 57:15 43
Isaiah 6:3 55
Isaiah 63:10-11 .... 38, 41
Isaiah 64:6 * KJV 118
Isaiah 66:22-24 145
Isaiah 7:14 158
Isaiah 9:6 52

J

James 1:13 .... 26, 51, 160
James 2:26 * 99
James 3:13-17 56
James 3:13-17 * 57, 120
James 4:1-10 169
James 4:1-8 * 124
James 4:5-7 * 117
James 4:6 169
James 5:20 144
Jeremiah 13:17 * KJV 111
Jeremiah 14:6 37

Jeremiah 17:9 * KJV 82	John 14:26 .... 39, 93
Jeremiah 26:13 49	John 14:26-27 * 92
Jeremiah 31:31-34 .... 91, 92, 155	John 14:3 * NIV 166
Jeremiah 31:31-34 * 92, 127	John 14:6 .... 127, 134
Jeremiah 4:19 * KJV 66	John 15 45
Jeremiah 49:36 37	John 15:1 * 89
Jeremiah 5:9, 29; 6:8; 9:9 68	John 15:26 46
Jeremiah 51:15 33	John 15:26 * 70
Jeremiah 9:24 * ix	John 16:13-15 * 83
Job 11:8 174	John 16:13-16 * 70
Job 13:17-28 35	John 16:7-15 * 90
Job 32:8 121	John 17:17 * 25
Job 33:16-18 105	John 17:2 91
Job 34:15 53	John 17:22-23 * 86
Job 38:1-13 * 88	John 17:25 55
Job 38:1-18 * 162	John 17:5 * 82
Job 4:9; 19:17 37	John 2:24 167
Job 40:1-14 * 163	John 20:29-31 * 170
Job 7:15 * KJV 66	John 3:16 .... 57, 107
John 1:1, 14 .... 145, 154	John 3:20 98
John 1:1-3 .... 32, 89	John 3:3 111
John 1:29 154	John 3:3-16 58
John 1:3 89	John 3:3-6 .... 83, 100
John 1:41, 4:25 172	John 3:8-12 42
John 1:48-50 75	John 4:24 42
John 10:24-25 170	John 5:19-23 * 89
John 10:27-30 * 91, 128	John 5:22-23 91
John 10:30 * 85, 89	John 5:28-29 * 101
John 11:1-16 82	John 5:29 145
John 11:24 101	John 5:45-46 85
John 11:25 134	John 8:27-29 * 82
John 11:35-37 * 85	John 8:44 115
John 12:14-16 155	John 8:44 * 56, 105
John 12:23-33 92	John 9:1-3 169
John 12:27 69	John 9:1-3 * NIV 167
John 12:32 91	Jonah 4:2 169
John 14:16-17 121	Jonah 4:5-11 51
John 14:16-17 * 70, 83	Joshua 10:12-14 51
John 14:16-17, 26; 16:8-11 128	Judges 10:16 68
John 14:2-3 * 76	

L

Leviticus 11:44-45 54
Leviticus 17:7 125
Leviticus 19:11 26
Leviticus 26:11, 30 68
Luke 1:26-38 158
Luke 1:32-33 172
Luke 1:46 * KJV 112
Luke 11:21-23 * 126
Luke 12:19 * KJV 66
Luke 13:1-5 50
Luke 13:22-28 133
Luke 16:22-26 131
Luke 16:22-31 174
Luke 16:23 145
Luke 17:13-19 169
Luke 19:41-42 * 85
Luke 2:10-11 * 154
Luke 2:14 50
Luke 2:25-32 91
Luke 20:42 155
Luke 22:3 44
Luke 22:39-46 * 73
Luke 22:42 * 89
Luke 22:44 46
Luke 24:44 .... 22, 91
Luke 4:1-13 * 159
Luke 4:41 .... 44, 125
Luke 4:43 * 92
Luke 5:20; 7:50; 17:19; 18:42 120
Luke 5:4-8 167
Luke 6:43 KJV 149
Luke 6:8 167
Luke 9:1-6 168

M

Malachi 3:6 .... 26, 51, 54, 173
Malachi 3:6 * 49
Mark 1:15 * 92
Mark 12:29 39
Mark 12:36 155
Mark 13:11 47
Mark 13:32 82
Mark 14:34 69
Mark 15:34 173
Mark 3:22 125
Mark 3:27 126
Mark 3:5 * 85
Mark 4:39 167
Mark 5:34; 10:52 120
Mark 6:20 55
Mark 7:20-22 105
Matthew 1:1-17 154
Matthew 1:18-25 158
Matthew 10:28 105
Matthew 10:38 * KJV 145
Matthew 12 45
Matthew 12:18 68
Matthew 12:22-28 166
Matthew 12:22-29 * 168
Matthew 12:26 126
Matthew 12:29 126
Matthew 12:40 174
Matthew 13:10-23 123
Matthew 13:31 99
Matthew 13:43-50 133
Matthew 14:24-28 166
Matthew 14:25 167
Matthew 15:10-20 * 114
Matthew 15:24-28 169
Matthew 16:18 39
Matthew 18 77
Matthew 18:20 77
Matthew 19:28 129
Matthew 2:5-6; 4:17 155
Matthew 21:4-10 155
Matthew 22:29-32 * 101
Matthew 22:44 155
Matthew 24:36 .... 50, 82
Matthew 25:32-46 101

Matthew 26:38 69
Matthew 28:18 91
Matthew 3:11; 12:32; 28:19 39
Matthew 4:23 154
Matthew 4:24; 8:16; 10:1 125
Matthew 5:1-13 44
Matthew 5:29; 13:41-43 145
Matthew 5:3 43
Matthew 6:30; 9:2; 9:22; 9:29;
    15:28; 17:20 120
Matthew 8:5-13 166
Matthew 9:44- 48 145
Matthew chapter 18 * 56
Micah 5:2 155

N

Numbers 11:16-17 164
Numbers 12:1-9 76
Numbers 12:1-9 * 72
Numbers 12:2 75
Numbers 12:5-8 * 88
Numbers 23:19 49
Numbers 32:14 * 84
Numbers 34:1-12 .... 92, 154
Numbers 5:14 * KJV 107

P

Philippians 1:19 46
Philippians 2:6-7 153
Proverbs 12:22 26
Proverbs 16:18, 19 43
Proverbs 16:2 38
Proverbs 16:5 * 117
Proverbs 2:6 * 57
Proverbs 21:24 105
Proverbs 23:7 * KJV 149
Proverbs 3:19-20 * 57
Proverbs 4:7 * 57
Proverbs 8:13 98
Psalm 103:19 * 161

Psalm 104:29 38
Psalm 104:5 53
Psalm 105:6-12 154
Psalm 105:8-12 92
Psalm 106:37 125
Psalm 11:5 68
Psalm 119:160 * 25
Psalm 119:17-24 231
Psalm 13:2 * KJV 66
Psalm 138:2 55
Psalm 139:7-10 * 50
Psalm 14:1-3 149
Psalm 14:3 115
Psalm 145:17 55
Psalm 147:4-5 * 113
Psalm 147:5 81
Psalm 16:10 174
Psalm 16:1-3 * KJV 111
Psalm 2:7 155
Psalm 25:8, 119:68 56
Psalm 3:8 121
Psalm 32:2 38
Psalm 33:19 144
Psalm 33:20 * KJV 66
Psalm 33:6 37
Psalm 34:6 75
Psalm 37:12-13 * 84
Psalm 5:4 .... 52, 98
Psalm 5:4 * 44
Psalm 51:11 41
Psalm 51:12 38
Psalm 51:1-3 149
Psalm 53:2-3 .... 108, 115
Psalm 53:2-3 * 106
Psalm 6:3 * KJV 66
Psalm 63:9 144
Psalm 68:18 175
Psalm 71:22; 99:9; 111:9 55
Psalm 78:69 53
Psalm 8:4-8 77

SCRIPTURE INDEX

Psalm 8:5 156
Psalms 110 155

R

Revelation 12:9 and 20:2 104
Revelation 14:9-13; 21:4 145
Revelation 15:4 55
Revelation 19:6-16 77
Revelation 2:16 50
Revelation 20 144
Revelation 20:11-15 130
Revelation 20:12-15 84
Revelation 20:12-15; 21:1-27 101
Revelation 20:13-14 174
Revelation 20:6; 20:14; 21:8 145
Revelation 21:2 55
Revelation 21:3-6 172
Revelation 21:4 .... 132, 133
Revelation 22:12 175
Romans 1:1-4 * NIV 156
Romans 1:16-17 154
Romans 1:18-20 54
Romans 1:20-21 * 33
Romans 1:3 NIV 156
Romans 1:8 120
Romans 10:17 * 119
Romans 11:15-24 .... 86, 107
Romans 11:25-27 27
Romans 11:25-33 127
Romans 12:1, 2 64
Romans 13:1-7 164
Romans 15:13 124
Romans 16:25 27
Romans 16:26 52
Romans 2:5-11 84
Romans 3:10-18 * 106
Romans 3:9-19 .... 45, 115
Romans 4:14 128
Romans 4:2-3 * 118
Romans 5:12 116
Romans 5:1-21 98
Romans 5:13-19 105
Romans 5:14 159
Romans 5:5-8 93
Romans 5:8-11 53
Romans 6:14-23 128
Romans 6:16-18 * 118
Romans 6:23 168
Romans 7:14-25 149
Romans 7:14-25, 12:1-2 124
Romans 8:10 105
Romans 8:15 28
Romans 8:15-16 121
Romans 8:21 53
Romans 8:26-27 * 47
Romans 8:26-28 169
Romans 8:28 51
Romans 8:34 77
Romans 8:9 45
Romans 8:9 * 45
Romans 9:14-15 * 85
Romans 9:15 169
Romans 9:20-21 * 162
Romans Chapter 8 45

T

Titus 1:2 26
Titus 2:3 118
Titus 3:4-8 56
Titus 3:5 .... 47, 129

Z

Zechariah 9:9 155

Study Guide Suggestions

The key to a good discussion is to start with the Preface and Introduction, which will provide you with some context for what you are reading. The key to my books is the Scriptures, which are the foundation for understanding God's truth, and I hope you find the following suggestions to be helpful.

1. Before each group meeting, you should assign a chapter for everyone to read.
2. Research the endnotes at the end of each chapter. The material and websites listed will offer additional information on the topics noted.
3. Read a paragraph or sub-title section aloud; pause for comments or questions.
4. Another option is to look up all the Scriptures as referenced, and see how they fit into the context of the subject being discussed. Then ask if these Scriptures are relevant, or how they may clarify the understanding of the topic or the concepts.
5. Other helpful questions may be: Is this information new to anyone? Is this important or relevant to my understanding of the Scriptures? Does this information offer a wider context for other important aspects of my understanding? Does this apply to other Scriptural concepts?
6. A good way to wrap up discussions on any segment is to ask others to summarize what has been said, within the book's contents, and within the discussion.

You may find these suggestions help you to discover other approaches to discussion groups. But your preferred choices are ultimately between you and the Holy Spirit, who is our ultimate teacher.

To quote the Apostle Paul: "The grace of the Lord Jesus Christ, and the love of God, and the fellowship of the Holy Spirit, be with you all." (2 Corinthians 13:14)

ACKNOWLEDGEMENTS

For any spiritual insight I may have displayed in this book, I want to thank God the Father for his plan for the Universe, God the Son for making the sacrifice and providing the way for the Father's plan, and God the Holy Spirit for carrying out the Father's plan through teaching and illuminating our souls for understanding (Psalm 119:17-24).

I want to express my deep appreciation to Jeremy Rosenberger for his help in the editing of both the first and revised editions of this book. Jeremy is a software architect and consultant who holds a B.S. degree in Computer Science and Engineering from Cornell University, and is a published author.

ABOUT THE AUTHOR

Reid Ashbaucher born in the United States, and holds a B.A. degree in Comprehensive Bible from Cedarville University, Cedarville, Ohio; an M.A. degree in Christian Theology from Trinity Theological Seminary, Newburgh, Indiana; and has completed some postgraduate work towards a Ph.D. in Religious Studies, endorsed by Canterbury Christ Church University, England.

Reid has been a believer in Jesus Christ for over 55 years. While experiencing life through secular fields of Military Service, Business Ownership and Radio Broadcast Engineering, Reid has served in local Christian churches as deacon, teacher and pulpit supply.

Throughout his life, Reid has sought to promote the Word of God as the source of true reality in all things. This reality can be summed up in Jesus Christ's words as He states: "Therefore everyone who hears these words of Mine, and acts upon them, may be compared to a wise man, who built his house upon the rock" (Matthew 7:24; NASB).

OTHER PUBLISHED WORKS BY THE AUTHOR

1. *Dispensational Theology: A Textbook on Eschatology in the Twenty-First Century* ISBN: 978-1-7331399-0-8 (pbk) ISBN: 978-1-7331399-1-5 (hbk)

2. *Christianity 101: A Simpler Way Forward*
   ISBN: 978-1-7331399-4-6 (pbk) ISBN: 978-1-7331399-5-3 (eBook)